# The Baptism
# of Fire

Personal Revival, Renewal
and the Anointing for
Supernatural Living

The Baptism of Fire
Personal Revival, Renewal and
The Anointing for Supernatural Living

Scripture quotations are taken from:
- NIV – The New International Version®. NIV®. Copyright © 1973, 1978, 1984 by International Bible Society. Used by permission of Zondervan. All rights reserved.
- NKJV – The New King James Version. Published by Thomas Nelson, Inc. Copyright © 1982 by Thomas Nelson, Inc. Used by permission. All rights reserved.
- AV – Authorised Version / King James Version.

ISBN 978-1-907066-56-6
British Library Cataloguing In Publication Data.
A Record of this Publication is available from the British Library.

First published in 2017 by ByFaith Media.

This book is also available as an ebook.

- Jesus Christ is Lord -

| **Page** | **Contents** | **Chapter** |
|---|---|---|

| Page | Contents | Chapter |
|------|----------|---------|

## Holy Spirit Bible Studies

# Introduction

A personal revival is possible! John the Baptist said of Jesus, "He will baptise you with the Holy Spirit and fire" (Matthew 3:11). Did you notice the two distinct baptisms outlined by John? Many have been baptised in the Holy Spirit, but how many have been baptised into God's fire?

The baptism of fire is a real experience with the Holy Spirit and you don't have to wait for others to be ready. It is something that can happen to you, if you want it. You can have a personal spiritual awakening, a renewal and revitalisation!

Many have experienced this baptism of fire and throughout this book there are testimonies of those who have walked closely with God through His fire. I call these people disciples of the Lord Jesus Christ. They were hungry for God and decided to move on with Him, regardless of others. They decided not to be held back in their relationship with God by religious structures, or unbiblical doctrines.

In the Bible we are given numerous examples of men and women of faith who walked closely with the Lord, who saw their lives transformed. Many received the baptism of the Spirit, others the baptism of fire and some were clothed with God's Spirit. Their lives teach us that the only restriction we have with moving on with God, is the restrictions we place upon ourselves through disobedience, indifference, or submission to empty religious tradition.

In this book, we will find how the Holy Spirit works in people's lives, what it costs to walk with God and how we can move on with Him. This book is filled with Scripture so that we can learn how the ministry of the Holy Spirit was outworked throughout the Bible and find how others abided in the presence of God.

To walk with the Lord by His Holy Spirit we must make room for Him. We have to be prepared to give up the empty loves in order to embrace the eternal love and fire of God. As with Elijah and Elisha, the baptism of fire will burn away the chaff.

As we will find, the baptism of fire is more than a one-off experience we can have with the Holy Spirit. It is an ongoing lifestyle of abiding in Him, as we allow the fire of God to burn away all He wants to remove, to fill us with His Spirit, in order to make us true disciples of the Lord Jesus Christ.

Everything that is worth having comes at a cost, so it is with the baptism of fire. As the missionary and martyr Jim Elliot said, "He is no fool who gives what he cannot keep, to gain what he cannot lose."

# Chapter One

## Meeting the Holy Spirit

"I used to think of the Holy Spirit as an influence – a mystical power or force," said a disciple of the Lord. "Back then we referred to Him as the Holy Ghost because of the older translations of the Bible, but we knew nothing of Him as a Person.

"When I became a Christian most of the emphasis in the churches was directed towards the Father and the Son, and the Spirit of God was a mystery to us. Most of us were ignorant of the work of the Spirit, but things began to change as God began to pour out His Holy Spirit in fulfilment of the prophecy of Joel (Acts 2:14-21).

"When I had my first encounter with the Holy Spirit He came as the Dove of peace and joy, and baptised me in Himself. How wonderful was His infilling of peace! Then He convicted me of sin, showing me I was 'bound' and 'poisoned' by my rebellion (Acts 18:23). He desired to make Jesus Christ my true Lord (1 Corinthians 12:3). He exposed much hypocrisy, selfishness and pride, all to help make me be conformed to the image of Christ (Romans 8:29).

"As the Holy Spirit began moving in the churches He showed us that He is also the Gift Giver (1 Corinthians 12:4-11). He came and dispersed the gifts of the Spirit to the believers He chose, and we were thrilled that He worked amongst us. But after many years, we realised that most of our experiences with God were still shallow and there had to be a deeper walk in Him (Ezekiel 47:3-5).

"Then, as I read of great Christian leaders from Church history, I discovered that many of them had deep and powerful relationships with God the Holy Spirit, just as the apostles had. Duncan Campbell (1898-1972), the Hebridean revivalist in the UK, witnessed the presence of the Spirit come down upon a community in such power that people fell down in the streets weeping under conviction of sin.

"Evan Roberts (1879-1951), sought God desperately for the presence of the Holy Spirit and the Lord came and met with him, and revival soon flowed in Wales, UK, and changed the nation.

"I learnt much from Rees Howells (1879-1950). God showed Him that the Spirit wants to come and live in and through us, like He did with the prophets and apostles. Rees Howells was taught by the Holy Spirit how to prevail in intercession and he was a channel for God's blessing to the world. He led countless thousands to the Lord, was an instrument used in revival, witnessed many healings and his prayers shaped world events. His ministry was so powerful that his biography touched the lives of millions of people! The secret to the powerful ministry Rees Howells exercised was that it was not him doing the work, but the Holy Spirit living in and through him.

"Through testimonies like these and many others from servants of God, it became clear to me that there is much more for us all to experience with God the Holy Spirit. Many of God's great servants from the past taught that it is possible to give oneself completely over to the Holy Spirit, and allow Him to come in and possess every area of one's life. This is what Paul wrote about concerning being filled with the fullness of God (Ephesians 3:19). These people experienced the baptism of fire!

"As I studied the teaching of Jesus Christ – the anointed One Himself – on the ministry of the Spirit, I learnt He told the disciples it was a good thing that He was going away, because the Holy Spirit would be our Teacher and Guide to continue Christ's ministry (John 14:25-28, 15:26-27). As I examined the New Testament, the Holy Spirit showed me it was He who led the early Church and sent people out: 'Then the Spirit said to Philip, "Go near and overtake this chariot" ' (Acts 8:29), and, "While Peter thought about the vision, the Spirit said to him, 'Behold, three men are seeking you. Arise therefore, go down and go with them, doubting nothing; for I have sent them' (Acts 10:19-20) and, 'As they ministered to the Lord and fasted, the Holy Spirit said, "Now separate to Me Barnabas and Saul for the work to which I have called them" ' (Acts 13:2).

"Through these revelations God began to speak to me and others about going deeper with Him. The Holy Spirit showed us that He is a Person, just as real and powerful as the Father and the Son. He showed us that He has a will and a distinct personality (Ephesians 4:30). As the Lord Jesus Christ opened our spiritual eyes, we understood through the Bible that the Holy Spirit had always been working in the lives of the prophets and apostles. He was the One sending people forth, speaking and guiding them into Jesus' truth.

"The lesson from the lives of great servants of God is that the Holy Spirit is God on earth, but He has no body to live through, therefore He pursues those who call Jesus their Lord, and asks them if they are willing to welcome Him into their lives, in all His fullness (Acts 5:32). The Holy Spirit is not God out there somewhere, but God with us and in us, if we welcome Him. He is Christ's representative on earth, equal in authority and power with the Father and the Son, and yet He gives way to Jesus and spends His time glorifying Christ (John 16:14), who then glorifies the Father (John 17:4). I once thought I knew a lot about God, but the Holy Spirit revealed to me that I do not know anything which I am not applying!"

*Questions to consider:* Are you prepared to go on a journey with Christ and discover the Holy Spirit as a Person?
*Actions:* Ask God's Holy Spirit to truly make Jesus your Lord.

# Chapter Two

## The Spirit Wrote the Bible with People's Lives

This is the first of a series of short Bible studies in this book, which highlight the work, ministry, power and Person of the Spirit of God.

- 'The Spirit of God was hovering over the face of the waters' (Genesis 1:2).
- "My Spirit shall not strive with man forever" (Genesis 6:3).
- "I have filled him with the Spirit of God in wisdom, in understanding, in knowledge and in all manner of workmanship" (Exodus 31:3).
- "Oh that all the Lord's people were prophets and that the Lord would put His Spirit upon them!" (Numbers 11:29).
- "Take Joshua the son of Nun with you, a man in whom is the Spirit" (Numbers 27:18).
- 'The Spirit of the Lord came upon him' (Judges 3:10).
- 'The Spirit of the Lord came upon Gideon' (Judges 6:34).
- 'The Spirit of the Lord came upon Jephthah' (Judges 11:29).
- 'The Spirit of God came mightily upon him' (Judges 14:6).
- 'Then the Spirit of God came upon him and he prophesied among them' (1 Samuel 10:10).
- 'The Spirit of the Lord came upon David from that day forward' (1 Samuel 16:13).
- 'Then the Spirit of God was upon him also and he went on and prophesied' (1 Samuel 19:20-23).
- "I will not hide My face from them anymore; for I shall have poured out My Spirit on the house of Israel" (Ezekiel 39:29).
- 'But truly I am full of power by the Spirit of the Lord, and of justice and might' (Micah 3:8).
- 'The mystery of Christ...has now been revealed by the Spirit to His holy apostles and prophets' (Ephesians 3:4-5).
- 'Of this salvation the prophets have inquired and searched...the Spirit of Christ who was in them was indicating when He testified beforehand the sufferings of Christ and the glories that would follow...have been reported to you through those who have preached the gospel to you by the Holy Spirit sent from heaven – things which angels desire to look into' (1 Peter 1:10-12).

## Chapter Three

## The Conviction and Seal of the Holy Spirit

In the Bible we learn that the Holy Spirit is our first contact with God. It is the Holy Spirit who reveals our sin to us, and He is the One who convicts us of our need to know God the Father, through His Son and our Saviour Jesus Christ. Jesus said, "When He has come, He will convict the world of sin and of righteousness, and of judgment" (John 16:8). The Holy Spirit is the Person who opens our eyes to the life of Jesus Christ – to His death, resurrection and ascension. Jesus taught that the Holy Spirit's conviction is essential for the salvation of the world (John 16:8-11).

When the Holy Spirit convicts us of sin, He will make us feel very uncomfortable on the inside. It could feel like our consciences have been set on fire or we may feel 'knotted' on the inside, as we realise how sinful we have been because of our unwillingness to yield to the Lord Jesus Christ.

Our response to the conviction of the Holy Spirit in our lives, will determine our eternal destiny. Christ died for our sins according to the Scriptures and it is the Holy Spirit who makes His sacrifice real to us. As the Holy Spirit convicts us, we get the choice to respond to His conviction and believe in Jesus Christ, or we can harden our hearts to Him, and continue to be religious and rebellious!

Jesus said, "Let not your heart be troubled; you believe in God, believe also in Me" (John 14:1), and the apostle Paul preached, "Believe on the Lord Jesus Christ, and you will be saved, you and your household" (Acts 16:31). Finally, God's promise to us is this: 'If you confess with your mouth the Lord Jesus and believe in your heart that God has raised Him from the dead, you will be saved' (Romans 10:9).

Rees Howells (1879-1950) was raised in a very religious community in Wales, UK. Practically everyone knew of the Saviour's life and most had a simple faith in Him. Christianity had penetrated the culture to such an extent that even worldly, sinful people observed the Sabbath and were aware of God's convicting power. Due to this very religious environment, which included regular chapel attendance, Rees Howells believed he was a 'good man,' even a 'Christian,' and he felt no need of any further commitment or experience with God.

However, Rees Howells did not realise he was in a state of rebellion against God, because he refused to yield to Christ's most important commandment, "You must be born again" (John 3:7).

Rees Howells was resisting the will and purposes of God for his life (Luke 7:30), and the Holy Spirit began to convict him by making him very uncomfortable within. "I believed in the Saviour," Rees Howells testified, "but one thing I knew, I wasn't born of Him. I was outside God's Kingdom, which all my good living and religious upbringing had never enabled me to enter, because I had no correspondence or relationship with God."

The Holy Spirit convicted Rees Howells that Christ was standing at the door of his heart and was asking to come in. "Behold I stand at the door and knock," he told Rees. "May I come in to you? Will you accept me?" Rees replied, "Yes," and in his words, "He came in, and that moment I changed. I was born again into another world. I found myself in the Kingdom of God, and the Creator became my Father. It wasn't a point of doctrine I saw, no, it was Calvary, and I saw Christ crucified and raised again, and I put my faith in Him. That night I received the gift of eternal life, that gift which money can never buy. The Saviour became everything to me. Everything of this world was rough, but everything about Him, so holy, pure and beautiful. I changed altogether. None of my old friends could understand what had happened."

Rees Howells' life of faith began when he responded to the conviction of the Holy Spirit, and it will be the same for us. Before we ever hear God saying, "Go," we must heed Him when He says, "No," to sin and, "Yes," to the Saviour and His will for our lives.

The first thing the Holy Spirit asks of us is to repent, turn away from our lives of sin and truly put our faith in Jesus Christ to become born again! When we allow Him to lead us into purging repentance, the Holy Spirit will honour our response to His conviction of sin, and we will receive a deposit of the Holy Spirit within us. We too will become truly born again by the Spirit of God (John 3:5-8). Paul explains this process when he wrote: 'Having believed, you were sealed with the Holy Spirit of promise' (Ephesians 1:13), and, 'Do not grieve the Holy Spirit of God, by whom you were sealed for the day of redemption' (Ephesians 4:30). This is the seal of the Spirit, but as Rees Howells and Evan Roberts found, it is not the baptism of the Spirit, nor the full-indwelling of the Holy Spirit.

Evan Roberts (1879-1951) was a young man who became the most prominent leader of the Welsh Revival (1904-1905). This revival is often credited as the most powerful revival in modern history. Evan Roberts urged all to respond to the conviction of the Holy Spirit and he laid out four points for all people to consider before they could meet with God the Holy Spirit, who comes to glorify Jesus.

"1. Is there any sin in your past with which you have not honestly dealt with, or not confessed to God? On your knees at once. Your past must be put away and cleansed.

"2. Is there anything in your life that is doubtful – anything which you cannot decide is good or evil? Away with it. There must not be a trace of a cloud between you and God. Have you forgiven everybody, everybody? If not, don't expect forgiveness for your sins (Matthew 18:34-35). Better to offend ten thousand friends than grieve the Spirit of God, or quench Him.

"3. Do what the Holy Spirit prompts without hesitation or fear. Obedience: prompt, implicit, unquestioning obedience at whatever cost.

"4. Make a public confession of Christ as your personal Saviour. Profession and confession are vastly different. Multitudes are guilty of long and loud profession. Confession of Christ as Lord has to do with His workings in your life today!"[1]

Both Rees Howells and Evan Roberts believed in the importance of purging repentance and faith in Jesus Christ, and they both emphasised the need for the Church to seek the Holy Spirit. But there is a danger today that well intentioned preachers use force of will to encourage people to believe in Christ, rather than allow the Holy Spirit to convict them of sin, leading to salvation.

"I remember seeing someone under conviction of sin," said a disciple of the Lord, "and I was so desperate to see him get saved, that I decided to talk to him and lead him in a prayer of faith in Christ. Years later I realised I had pushed this person ahead of God and did not allow the Holy Spirit to truly convict him of sin. His spiritual birth was premature and his faith died. I tried to do the Holy Spirit's work! Many still do the same in evangelism today."

In 1922, the evangelist Gipsy Smith speaking on Acts 16:30-32 said, "The truth is, we have preached a cheap religion far too long. We have cheapened Calvary in our thoughts, but it has never been cheapened with God. We have preached love until the people are lovesick. Salvation did not begin so much in the love of God as it did in the holiness of God. I want to make this truth very plain, very emphatic. It is good theology. Salvation comes from the holy Father, who hates sin, but who loves you. He hates your sin, but loves you. He gave His Son to make it possible for you to be saved. Your faith is a mockery if you still cherish your sin. Your faith is false if it does not mean absolute surrender."[2]

If the Holy Spirit does not work in and through the Church to convict people of sin and lead them to live like Christ, it will automatically move in the flesh (Romans 7:18). When a church does not have the Holy Spirit, it is dead. Therefore, it will seek for its relevance by maintaining laws and rules for its members. So often churches think they can do the job of reaching the world without the Holy Spirit, but without the Spirit of God there is no conviction of sin, and thus no real conversions. When this is the case, the churches become filled with people who have lip-synced a prayer of faith, but are not born again. Like parrots, they repeat words they do not understand or mean. As they are still in a state of rebellion to God, these people will reject all who come to them with the message of the Spirit. Churches without the Holy Spirit will often begin to openly persecute believers who have received the Spirit. This is a principle found in Scripture. 'As he who was born according to the flesh then persecuted him who was born according to the Spirit, even so it is now' (Galatians 4:29). As Jesus said, "These people draw near to Me with their mouth and honour Me with their lips, but their heart is far from Me. And in vain they worship Me" (Matthew 15:8-9). Paul left a warning to all believers to continue to live by the Spirit of God: 'Are you so foolish? Having begun in the Spirit, are you now being made perfect by the flesh?' (Galatians 3:3).

John Wesley (1703-1791), the English revivalist and founder of Methodism, went out as a missionary to reach North American Indians with Christ, but on his journey discovered he was not even born again himself! This is often the case today. Premature births in our churches are a reoccurring experience, which take place because we have watered-down the requirements to become born again. The requirements for a sincere new birth experience were noted in 1894 by Rev. B. Fay Mills: "There are four things to which he must be led if his salvation shall be complete," he preached. "The first is the renunciation of every known sin. Never speak one word of peace to an inquirer until you are sure he is willing to give up every known sin. The second is the consecration of the neutral things and the good things to God. He must be willing to put at the disposal of God his time, money, influence, ambition, pleasures, friends etc. In the third place, he must see that he must depend entirely upon Christ for the cleansing of his heart and his preservation in the path of life. In the fourth place he must be willingly open to confess Christ as his Master. Never call the work done until these four things have been accomplished."[3]

"It is the Holy Spirit who convicts us of sin and leads us to faith in Christ," said a disciple of the Lord Jesus Christ. "Then I believe there are three keys to fruitful Christian living. The first is total surrender to the Lord, giving the Holy Spirit the right to come and live in you, just as Jesus would – to convict and guide.

"The second key is explicit and unconditional obedience to God whatever the cost. What is the point of partial obedience? With partial obedience, you will leave Egypt hoping for an abundant life and you will get stuck half way into the desert and wait there!

"The third key is endless endurance. Never give up on the Lord's call! We must endure and walk through the desert to the Promised Land. Without inner endurance, Satan will know all he has to do is keep battling and wait for you to give up. If you endure you will receive the reward of faithfulness! (Matthew 24:13, Hebrews 11:6).

"These are three great keys. What will you do with them? Surrender to Him, obey Him, and endure with Him – three simple truths that take a lifetime to learn!"

In this book, we are constantly considering the need for the Holy Spirit and the necessity to give ourselves to the Holy Spirit, but we never exclude the other members of the Trinity, because the Father, Son and Holy Spirit are One. The Father draws us (John 6:44), the Son saves us (Acts 2:38, 3:19, 4:12, Romans 5:8), and the Holy Spirit convicts us of sin (John 16:16). It was the Father who sent the Son and the Son sent the Holy Spirit (John 3:16, 16:7). To get to know the Father we need to go through the Door of the Son, and the Holy Spirit then seals and regenerates us (John 3:3, 7, John 14:7, 2 Timothy 2:19). The Holy Spirit bears witness that we are children of God (John 1:12, John 15:26), and we can only be saved after we have responded to the call of 'the Spirit,' and have come in repentance (Matthew 3:2, 4:17, Revelation 22:17). Paul was sent by Jesus, "To open their eyes, in order to turn them from darkness to light, and from the power of Satan to God, that they may receive forgiveness of sins and an inheritance among those who are sanctified by faith in Me" (Acts 26:18).

"What is missing in our churches today?" asked a disciple of the Lord. "For many people it is purging repentance and a life-changing born again experience. Jesus said, 'That which is born of the flesh is flesh and that which is born of the Spirit is spirit' (John 3:5-8). We need the Spirit of God to birth Christ in us (1 Peter 1:23). Too many people have been told, 'You're now a Christian,' despite the fact that they have never been broken before the convicting power of the Spirit of God. It is He who convicts us of sin, shows us our need for the Saviour and opens our eyes to see that Jesus is the Door to God the Father (John 10:7). Through Jesus we have access by the Spirit to the Father (Ephesians 2:18), and He who has the Son has the Father (1 John 2:23). We need the Spirit more than we know. The foundations for the baptism of fire are laid when we face the full implications of the call to discipleship!"

*Questions to consider:* Have you had a premature birth of faith? Have you allowed the Holy Spirit to convict you of sin? Have you experienced purging repentance and put your faith solely in Christ?

*Actions:* Spend some time seeking God on your own and humble yourself. Open your heart to listen to the conviction of the Holy Spirit. Reject all religious self-confidence and put your faith solely in Christ's death and resurrection. Trust in Him alone, with humility of heart and ask for the gift of purging repentance.

# Chapter Four

## The Spirit and the Prophets

- "The Spirit of the Lord spoke by me and His Word was on my tongue" (2 Samuel 23:2).
- "The Spirit of the Lord will carry you to a place I do not know" (1 Kings 18:12).
- 'Then the Spirit came upon Amasai and he said, "We are yours, O David. We are on your side, O son of Jesse! Peace, peace to you and peace to your helpers! For your God helps you" ' (1 Chronicles 12:18).
- 'Now the Spirit of God came upon Azariah the son of Oded, and he went out to meet Asa and said to him, "Hear me...the Lord is with you while you are with Him" ' (2 Chronicles 15:1-2).
- 'Then the Spirit of God came upon Zechariah the son of Jehoiada the priest, who stood above the people and said to them, "Thus says God, 'Why do you transgress the commandments of the Lord so that you cannot prosper?' " ' (2 Chronicles 24:20).
- 'You also gave Your good Spirit to instruct them' (Nehemiah 9:20).
- 'Yet for many years You had patience with them and testified against them by Your Spirit in Your prophets' (Nehemiah 9:30).
- "Woe to the rebellious children," says the Lord, "who take counsel, but not of Me and who devise plans, but not of My Spirit, that they may add sin to sin" (Isaiah 30:1).
- "The Spirit is poured upon us from on high and the wilderness becomes a fruitful field" (Isaiah 32:15).
- "For My mouth has commanded it and His Spirit has gathered them" (Isaiah 34:16).
- "For I will pour water on him who is thirsty and floods on the dry ground; I will pour My Spirit on your descendants, and My blessing on your offspring. They will spring up among the grass like willows by the watercourses" (Isaiah 44:3-4).
- "I will put My Spirit within you and cause you to walk in My statutes" (Ezekiel 36:27).
- "I will put My Spirit in you and you shall live" (Ezekiel 37:14).
- "Is the Spirit of the Lord restricted?" (Micah 2:7).
- "I will pour out My Spirit on all flesh..." (Joel 2:28).
- "This is the Word of the Lord to Zerubbabel, 'Not by might nor by power, but by My Spirit,' says the Lord of hosts" (Zechariah 4:6).

# Chapter Five

## The Baptism of the Holy Spirit

The baptism of the Holy Spirit can mean different things to various people and denominations, but in the context of this book, we are returning to what Jesus taught about the work of the Holy Spirit. Jesus said, "Whoever drinks of the water that I shall give him will never thirst. But the water that I shall give him will become in him a fountain of water springing up into everlasting life" (John 4:14). Do you have this living water flowing within you?

The disciples of Jesus were converted and received the seal of the Spirit when Jesus breathed on them saying, "Receive the Holy Spirit" (John 20:22). Nevertheless, this was not the end. They did not receive all there was to receive, because Jesus also told them to, "Tarry in the city of Jerusalem," and wait "for the promise of My Father" (Luke 24:49). Many Christians are in a similar position, Jesus has breathed on them and they were sealed with the Spirit at conversion (Ephesians 1:13), but they have not tarried in their Jerusalem to be baptised in the Holy Spirit, as the apostles did in Acts 2:1-4. Being sealed by the Spirit is conversion, being baptised in the Spirit is immersion – it's like meeting the Person for the first time and feeling His love, joy and peace. It's another world. Being baptised in God's fire is a further step!

In the Great Commission to make disciples of all nations, Jesus stated that His followers would drive out demons, speak with new tongues and heal the sick (Mark 16:17-18). All of this is impossible without the baptism of the Holy Spirit. This is one of the reasons why some Christians have never been involved with expelling demons, healing the sick or speaking in tongues, because they have not received the baptism of the Holy Spirit, to fulfil the command of Jesus in Mark 16:15-18. These signs will follow, in the words of Jesus, "Those who believe." The power of the Holy Spirit is not for special ministers, but for all who believe!

Jesus said to them, "Go into all the world and preach the gospel to all creation...and these signs will accompany those who believe: In My name they will drive out demons; they will speak in new tongues; they will pick up snakes with their hands; and when they drink deadly poison, it will not hurt them at all; they will place their hands on sick people and they will get well" (Mark 16:15, 17-18).

D.L. Moody (1837-1899), a famous evangelist preached about the dangers of making 'good church goers' without directing people to their need of the Holy Spirit. "If a man is only converted and we get him into the Church, we think the work is done," said Moody, "and we let him get right off to sleep, instead of urging him to seek the gift of the Holy Ghost (The Holy Spirit), that he may be anointed for the work...the world would soon be converted if all such were baptised with the Holy Ghost." This conviction of Moody's was grounded in his own experience with God the Holy Spirit.

Moody had the largest congregation in Chicago, USA, but some godly women told him, "We've been praying for you, because you need power!" He was offended by their comments as he had reasonable success in the ministry; but in his own words: "Their earnest talk about the 'power of the Holy Spirit and His anointing' set me thinking. I asked them to come and talk with me, and we got down on our knees. They poured out their hearts that I might receive the anointing with the Holy Spirit and there came a great hunger into my soul. I knew not what it was. I began to cry as never before. The hunger increased. I really felt I did not want to live any longer if I could not have this power. I kept on crying all the time that God would fill me with the Holy Spirit. Well, one day, in the city of New York, oh, what a day! I cannot describe it...I can only say God revealed Himself to me, and I had such an experience of His love and power, of the Holy Spirit, that I had to ask Him to stay His hand. I went again to preaching. The sermons were not different; I did not present any new truths and yet hundreds were converted."[1]

Evangelist and revivalist, the Rev. Lionel B. Fletcher stated in 1931 that after his conversion, the greatest experience he ever had, was when he realised 'the mighty gift of the Holy Ghost was not only for men of the New Testament days, but was available for men today...the Christian's birthright is the power of the Holy Ghost.'[2]

One of the great deceptions in Church history is the satanic doctrine that the baptism of the Holy Spirit, and the miracles or gifts of the Spirit were only for the apostles. To inspire this doctrine, Satan had penetrated the minds of theologians who interpreted the Bible by their experiences, rather than bringing their experiences up to the level of the Bible! Therefore, they declared that the book of Acts and accounts of the work of the Spirit in the New Testament could not be used to draw lessons from, and the experiences of the apostles were only for the first century. However, the Bible is very clear that: 'All Scripture is given by inspiration of God, and is profitable for doctrine, for reproof, for correction, for instruction in righteousness' (2 Timothy 3:16). Thus all the apostles' experiences have been recorded in Scripture by God, so we can learn from them and experience similar things! (Romans 15:4, 1 Corinthians 10:11).

William Fetler was used powerfully by God in Russia and his testimony was included in a 1933 book by Oswald J. Smith: "For the first time in my life I realised that the gift of the Holy Spirit had to be treated not only historically, but also experimentally; and that often our theological knowledge falls short of our theological practice. Then and there I prayed. By simple faith I claimed the promise of the Father. It meant breaking with every known sin. It meant full surrender to the Lord. It meant death and resurrection with the Saviour. The subsequent ministry in Russia proved the reality of that experience in London. Faith became the substance of things hoped for. God was faithful to His promise, showing that He is a rewarder of them that diligently seek Him."[3]

The promise of the baptism of the Holy Spirit for all believers from every generation began with Jesus Christ. John the Baptist speaking of Christ said, He "will baptise you with the Holy Spirit and fire" (Matthew 3:11, Mark 1:8, Luke 3:16), and, "Upon whom you see the Spirit descending and remaining on Him, this is He who baptises with the Holy Spirit" (John 1:33).

In the Old Testament, the Holy Spirit came upon Joel and he prophesied the will and promise of the Father stating: "I will pour out My Spirit on all flesh" (Joel 2:28-29). Jesus told His disciples that the time of this outpouring would begin soon when He said, "Behold, I send the Promise of My Father upon you; but tarry in the city of Jerusalem until you are endued with power from on high" (Luke 24:49, Acts 2:1-4). Then the apostles recalled what He required of them. 'He commanded them not to depart from Jerusalem, but to wait for the Promise of the Father, "which," He said, "you have heard from Me, for John truly baptised with water, but you shall be baptised with the Holy Spirit not many days from now" ' (Acts 1:4-5).

If the disciples had received all there was to receive at conversion, there would have been no need for them to wait for more, but just as they had to seek more from God, so must we. As the apostles waited upon God in prayer the promise was fulfilled in their lives. 'They were all filled with the Holy Spirit and began to speak with other tongues, as the Spirit gave them utterance' (Acts 2:4).

The first outpouring of the Spirit led to them speaking in tongues, and enabled a great revival to take place. But this was not a one-off experience, as later they received a further baptism in the Holy Spirit. 'They were all filled with the Holy Spirit and they spoke the Word of God with boldness' (Acts 4:31). Therefore, Christians do not receive the Holy Spirit 'just' once, and then never have another experience with Him. Instead we should come again and again to Him, until we have been completely filled with the Holy Spirit!

*Questions to consider:* Have you experienced the baptism of the Holy Spirit? Have you been endued with power from on high?

*Actions:* Open your life to the Holy Spirit and ask the Father to fulfil His promise to baptise you with Himself.

# Chapter Six

## Jesus' Promise of the Spirit

### The Need of the Holy Spirit

- Jesus answered, "Most assuredly, I say to you, unless one is born of water and the Spirit, he cannot enter the Kingdom of God. That which is born of the flesh is flesh and that which is born of the Spirit is spirit. Do not marvel that I said to you, 'You must be born again' " (John 3:5-7).
- Jesus said, "The wind blows where it wishes, and you hear the sound of it, but cannot tell where it comes from and where it goes. So is everyone who is born of the Spirit" (John 3:8).
- Jesus cried out, saying, "If anyone thirsts, let him come to Me and drink. He who believes in Me, as the Scripture has said, out of his heart will flow rivers of living water." But this He spoke concerning the Spirit, whom those believing in Him would receive; for the Holy Spirit was not yet given, because Jesus was not yet glorified' (John 7:37-39).
- Jesus said, "But the hour is coming, and now is, when the true worshipers will worship the Father in spirit and truth; for the Father is seeking such to worship Him. God is Spirit and those who worship Him must worship in spirit and truth" (John 4:23-24).

### The Promise of the Holy Spirit to be Claimed

- Jesus said, "So I say to you, ask and it will be given to you, seek and you will find, knock and the door will be opened to you. For everyone who asks receives; the one who seeks finds and to the one who knocks, the door will be opened. Which of you fathers, if your son asks for a fish, will give him a snake instead? Or if he asks for an egg, will give him a scorpion? If you then, though you are evil, know how to give good gifts to your children, how much more will your Father in heaven give the Holy Spirit to those who ask Him?" (Luke 11:9-13).
- Jesus said, "Whoever drinks the water I give them will never thirst. Indeed, the water I give them will become in them a spring of water welling up to eternal life" (John 4:14).
- 'You do not have because you do not ask God…You ask and do not receive, because you ask amiss, that you may spend it on your pleasures' (James 4:2-3).

## Chapter Seven

## Did You Receive Everything?

The primary sin of Satan, which led to him falling as an angel of God to become His adversary was pride (Ezekiel 28:13-17). At the heart of this sin, is the desire to be independent from God and for this reason pride is the sin which can destroy Christians. The Bible is filled with references to the need for humility, because God resists the proud. The proud do not need the Holy Spirit, they do not need to weep on their own before God, they do not need to cry out to God for help. The proud do not need to abide in Christ, daily receiving strength, guidance and instruction. The proud resist God.

One of the great distorted versions of pride in the Church is the statement, "I received everything at conversion!" How proud we have become. We prayed one prayer and immediately we were completely healed, our minds were renewed, and we received all there is to receive from God! Be careful...this is pride; it is the anti-God state of mind. When we were converted, we may have received every blessing in the heavenly realms in Christ, but we don't live there yet and there is much work to be done in us by the Spirit.

Let us return to the apostles. Did they receive everything at conversion or did they continually seek God, needing to walk closely with Christ, and know the Person of the Holy Spirit?

The apostles recorded three of their powerful experiences with the Holy Spirit (John 20:22, Acts 2:4, 4:31). Before this, Jesus' anointing rested on them when He sent them out in ministry (Luke 10:1-20). Later we find them continually 'praying in the Holy Spirit' and seeking God, as we shall find in later Bible studies.

How does the Holy Spirit come upon people? When the Holy Spirit came upon the apostles they were meeting together in prayer and worship, and the Spirit fell upon them. Later, the Holy Spirit was received by the laying on of hands: 'They sent Peter and John to them, who, when they had come down, prayed for them that they might receive the Holy Spirit...then they laid hands on them, and they received the Holy Spirit' (Acts 8:14-17).

The apostle Paul, the most prominent of all the apostles received the Spirit when Ananias laid his hands on him. 'Ananias...laying his hands on him said, "Brother Saul, the Lord Jesus, who appeared to you on the road as you came, has sent me that you may receive your sight and be filled with the Holy Spirit" ' (Acts 9:17).

Some Christians have been confused by Bible teachers who have not fully understood the teaching of the Scriptures, when they state that we receive everything at conversion; they have not studied and understood the experience of all the apostles. We shall return to this point again because it is very important. Jesus breathed on the disciples and said, "Receive the Holy Spirit" (John 20:22), and they were converted and sealed with the Spirit (2 Corinthians 5:5). But Jesus Christ also commanded them to wait in Jerusalem for the Spirit to indwell them (Luke 24:49, Acts 2:4).

Paul had a similar experience of conversion first, then baptism in the Holy Spirit later. Paul was saved and sealed (Acts 9:1-6), and then three days later received the baptism of the Holy Spirit (Acts 9:9, 17). Paul later wrote of the conversion experience: 'Having believed, you were sealed with the Spirit of promise' (Ephesians 1:13), and 'do not grieve the Holy Spirit of God, by whom you were sealed for the day of redemption' (Ephesians 4:30). Writing of this seal of the Spirit he confirmed: 'If anyone does not have the Spirit of Christ, he is not His' (Romans 8:9).

"The Bible states that God gives us a deposit of His Holy Spirit to seal us for the day of redemption," said a disciple of the Lord (2 Corinthians 5:5, Ephesians 4:30). "A deposit is a partial payment and this is what God gives us when we are born again (John 3:6). He seals us and gives us a taste of Himself, and then He waits to see how hungry we are for Him. Will we taste and see that the Lord is good or will we fold our arms and become stiff-necked to resist Him? (Psalm 34:8, Acts 7:51). When we accepted Jesus as Saviour we received a down-payment, now we must seek Him for the full inheritance, as sons and heirs" (Galatians 4:7).

International Bible teacher Gwen Shaw (1925-2013), taught that everyone needs the baptism of the Holy Spirit and without Him, we can do nothing. For this reason, Satan will try to keep us in pride, making us believe we can live without Him. She wrote: 'I believe Satan himself has fought this truth (of the baptism of the Spirit), because he knows that without the power of the Holy Spirit we are a Church that will exist in disunity, disarray and be powerless against evil. Without the Holy Spirit we are nothing.'[1]

The Holy Spirit cannot be contained or confined to one particular form of expression, therefore when Peter was preaching Christ to the Gentiles the Holy Spirit fell upon all those who heard the Word and they spoke in new heavenly tongues. 'While Peter was still speaking these words, the Holy Spirit fell upon all those who heard the Word and those of the circumcision who believed were astonished, as many as came with Peter, because the gift of the Holy Spirit had been poured out on the Gentiles also. For they heard them speak with tongues and magnify God' (Acts 10:44-46).

The apostles were amazed as they heard that the Holy Spirit was being given to all believers, from every background. "As I began to speak, the Holy Spirit fell upon them, as upon us at the beginning," testified Peter. "Then I remembered the Word of the Lord, how He said, 'John indeed baptised with water, but you shall be baptised with the Holy Spirit' " (Acts 11:15-16).

When Paul preached Christ, he also immediately laid his hands on those who believed and prayed for them. The new converts spoke in unknown heavenly tongues and prophesied, as the gifts of the Spirit were manifested amongst them (Acts 19:5-6).

Based on his experiences with the Spirit and the revelation he received from God, Paul began to write to the early Christians and explain the theological basis for receiving the Holy Spirit. First we are convicted of sin by the Holy Spirit (John 16:8), and if we repent and receive Christ, we are sealed by the Spirit (Ephesians 1:13). Then follows the baptism of the Spirit and surrender of every area of our lives, until we are truly filled with God. The baptism of fire! When Paul wrote to believers about 'being filled' with the Holy Spirit, in the original Greek it means to 'keep on being filled constantly and continually.'

As already explained, to claim we received all at conversion is a manifestation of pride. To free ourselves from this pride, we have to acknowledge the truth by examining our spiritual lives with a few questions: Was my mind renewed at conversion? Was I completely healed at conversion? Did I live a completely holy life after conversion? When we acknowledge our failure and need in humility, we find God's mercy (James 4:6). The religious leaders in Christ's day were judged by Him because they believed they already had it all and knew it all (Matthew 15:1-14). When we humble ourselves before God, we recognise our need and seek Him for more of Himself. Complete and unending total reliance on God is the hallmark of the kind of faith we need. As soon as we start believing 'we have it all,' we shall be disappointed and deceived (Acts 8:14-17). If we had it all – would we still behave as we do?

In 1903, Evan Roberts was a young unknown man who realised his great need for the baptism of the Holy Spirit. He gave himself to unceasing prayer for the Spirit of God to meet with Him, and he claimed the promises of the baptism of the Spirit from Scripture. He attended every meeting he could and testified, "I said to myself: I will have the Spirit and through all weathers and in spite of all difficulties I went to the meetings...for ten or eleven years I have prayed for revival. I could sit up all night to read or talk about revivals. It was the Spirit who moved me to think about revival....For a long, long time I was much troubled in my soul and my heart by thinking over the failure of Christianity. Oh! It seemed such a failure – such a failure – and I prayed and prayed, but nothing seemed to give me any relief. But one night, after I had been in great distress praying about this, I went to sleep and at one o'clock in the morning suddenly I was wakened up out of my sleep, and I found myself with unspeakable joy and awe in the very presence of the Almighty God! And for the space of four hours I was privileged to speak face to face with Him, as a man speaks face to face with a friend. At five o'clock it seemed to me as if I again returned to earth."

We may not have the same wonderful experiences that Evan Roberts had, but as often is the case with God, the deeper our cry, the greater the response will be. If you have not received the baptism of the Spirit, you can get on your knees, lift up your hands to God in prayer and cry out for Him to meet you. You may also find other faithful Christians to lay hands on you, and pray for you to receive the Spirit of God, such as happened to Paul (Acts 9:9, 17). The promise is real: "For everyone who asks receives, and he who seeks finds, and to him who knocks it will be opened" (Matthew 7:8).

It is important to remember that the baptism of the Holy Spirit is not 'just' another blessing to receive. When we receive the baptism of the Holy Spirit, we are welcoming a Person into our lives. That Person is God Himself, the Third member of the Trinity and He should have an enormous influence upon our lives – from the inside out!

When we invite a new person into our lives, we have to make room for him. If the individual is a holy person, we learn that our lifestyles may be offensive to him. Therefore we become sensitive to the individual's holy standards and we begin to "put off" our former conduct when in his presence. With this in mind, imagine what it would mean to invite the holiest Person on the planet into our lives! The Father and Jesus are in heaven, but on earth there is only one Person who is called "Holy," and He wants to dwell in our bodies! If godly people can influence us to live better lives, imagine what it would mean to invite the holiest Person on earth into our lives!

When we honestly invite this holy Person to live in us, we will have to 'make room' for Him. In fact, He will want us to have a continual clear-out of all sin, self and worldliness! His influence upon us should be more powerful than any influence from any other person, because He will be living in us! The world presses us to conform to its standards from the outside, the Holy Spirit presses us to conform to the image of Christ from the inside (Romans 8:29-30).

Whilst attending a conference in which he fully gave himself to God, the soul winner Archdeacon Tress of Sydney, Australia said, "God can only fill us to the extent that we yield ourselves to Him. If you yield yourself without reserve to God, you have the right to know that God gives Himself without reserve to you, and by faith you may claim the filling of the Holy Ghost."[2]

Now what are you waiting for? You need to be baptised in the Holy Spirit! In 1906, the Rev. Evan Hopkins, the preacher who inspired Rees Howells to seek the Holy Spirit at the Llandrindod Convention, in Wales, UK, said believers in Jesus should never hesitate. "You can yield at once," he said. "Oh, but then I always thought that if I have to be filled with the Spirit, I have to wait...wait! Wait for the Spirit? Where is the Spirit? He came down at Pentecost, to the Church. Why should you wait for the Spirit?"[3]

"Before I was baptised in the Holy Spirit my Christian life was very shallow," said a disciple of the Lord. "I believed in Jesus, yet I did not have a real relationship with Him. I read the Bible and none of it seemed alive to me. The world appeared alive to me, because I was still controlled by my flesh. Then, when I received the baptism in the Holy Spirit, suddenly a cloud lifted from me, a peace descended and arose within me, and the Bible became alive. The same passages that once seemed dull and dusty spoke into my life. Before I had read the Bible, now the Bible reads me.

"Then I read about the disciples and how hard they had tried to follow the Lord, and how they had failed. That was like me. But the Holy Spirit came upon them and they were filled with fire and changed from within! That can happen to anyone. It can happen to you! Has it happened to you yet?

"There are several principles in the Bible for all to follow to receive the Holy Spirit.

"The first is to ask on the basis of Jesus' promise in Luke 11:13.

"The second is to obey the Lord in accordance with Acts 5:32.

"The third is to seek the Lord until He comes upon you. The disciples had to wait for God to send His Spirit, but now the Spirit has been sent – God may be waiting on you! But don't worry if you have to pray a while before He comes, perhaps He's testing your sincerity and perseverance (Luke 24:49).

"The fourth is to believe His promise (Galatians 3:14).

"Finally, if the Holy Spirit does not come to meet you on your own, the fifth principle is to seek out Spirit filled believers and ask for them to pray for you to be baptised in the Holy Spirit as Paul had to" (Acts 9:17).

*Questions to consider:* Have you experienced the baptism of the Holy Spirit? Have you humbled yourself and set time aside, to seek God to endue you with power from on high?

*Actions:* Open your life to the Holy Spirit and ask the Father to fulfil His promise to baptise you with the Holy Spirit. If you don't have enough faith to seek God on your own, find other believers who have experienced the baptism of the Holy Spirit, and ask them to lay hands on you to pray, just as it happened to the apostle Paul.

# Chapter Eight

## Sealed and Filled

### Sealed by the Holy Spirit and Waiting for More!

- 'When He had said this, He breathed on them and said to them, "Receive the Holy Spirit" ' (John 20:22).
- Jesus said, "That which is born of the flesh is flesh and that which is born of the Spirit is spirit" (John 3:6).
- Jesus said, "For John truly baptised with water, but you shall be baptised with the Holy Spirit not many days from now" (Acts 1:5).
- Jesus said, "You shall receive power when the Holy Spirit has come upon you; and you shall be witnesses to Me in Jerusalem, in all Judea and Samaria, and to the end of the earth" (Acts 1:8).
- "I will pour out My Spirit on all flesh; your sons and your daughters shall prophesy, your young men shall see visions, your old men shall dream dreams, and on My menservants and on My maidservants I will pour out My Spirit in those days, and they shall prophesy" (Acts 2:17-18).
- 'Now He who establishes us with you in Christ and has anointed us is God, who also has sealed us and given us the Spirit in our hearts as a guarantee' (2 Corinthians 1:21-22).
- 'Now He who has prepared us for this very thing is God, who also has given us the Spirit as a guarantee' (2 Corinthians 5:5).
- 'Now the Lord is the Spirit and where the Spirit of the Lord is, there is liberty. But we all, with unveiled face, beholding as in a mirror the glory of the Lord, are being transformed into the same image from glory to glory, just as by the Spirit of the Lord' (2 Corinthians 3:17-18).
- 'When you believed, you were marked in Him with a seal, the promised Holy Spirit, who is a deposit guaranteeing our inheritance until the redemption of those who are God's possession, to the praise of His glory' (Ephesians 1:13-14).
- 'When the kindness and the love of God our Saviour toward man appeared, not by works of righteousness which we have done, but according to His mercy He saved us, through the washing of regeneration and renewing of the Holy Spirit' (Titus 3:4-5).
- 'The one who keeps God's commands lives in Him and He in them. And this is how we know that He lives in us: We know it by the Spirit He gave us' (1 John 3:24).

# Chapter Nine

## The Person of the Holy Spirit

Evan Roberts had wonderful encounters with God as he sought the Lord in prayer at night, yet he still needed to be baptised in the Holy Spirit before revival came to Wales, UK, in 1904. Evan Roberts was listening to Seth Joshua preaching one day, when he heard him praying, "Lord, bend us," in Welsh. When fully translated into English, the prayer indicates total submission to God, a breaking of the will and a humbling before Him. The Holy Spirit said to Evan, "That's what you need," and he began to pray for this breaking, bending and total submission to God in desperation.

In the next meeting the Holy Spirit came and met Evan Roberts. "I felt a living power pervading my bosom," he testified. "It took my breath away and my legs trembled exceedingly. This living power became stronger and stronger as each one prayed, until I felt it would tear me apart. My whole bosom was in turmoil and if I had not prayed it would have burst...I fell on my knees with my arms over the seat in front of me. My face was bathed in perspiration and the tears flowed in streams. I cried out, 'Bend me, bend me!' It was God's commending love which bent me...what a wave of peace flooded my bosom...I was filled with compassion for those who must bend at the judgment and I wept. Following that, the salvation of the human soul was solemnly impressed on me. I felt ablaze with the desire to go through the length and breadth of Wales to tell of the Saviour."

Revival soon followed and as many as 250,000 people could have been converted during the 1904-1905 revival, out of a population of just one million![1] Nevertheless, most of the Christian leaders were unfamiliar with the leading of the Holy Spirit, and did not know how to teach discipleship to the converts and there was backsliding.

After this revival, Rees Howells realised many people had been convicted and blessed by the Holy Spirit, but they had not been completely filled with the fullness of God (Ephesians 3:19). Rees, with other young believers at the time, felt powerless to help these new Christians who were falling away from Christ.

In Rees' heart, there was a deep sense there must be something deeper to experience, than the personal reviving of one's faith, and one day whilst he listened to the Rev. Evan Hopkins, he suddenly realised that even though he had fallen in love with the Saviour, he had at the same time been ignorant of the One whom the Saviour said would continue His ministry on earth (John 16:7-15).

As he grew older, Rees Howells began to learn that the blessing of the presence of the Holy Spirit is an experience we can all have, but after this blessing, we still need to be prepared to meet the Person!

Rees Howells was listening to the Rev. Evan Hopkins at the Llandrindod Convention, who was speaking on the Holy Spirit when Hopkins said, "He is the personal Holy Ghost; not a mere influence, but the Spirit of God, equal with the Father and the Son. Give a reception to the Holy Ghost. He is not far off, He is close to you. You have not to wait for Him, but you have to wake up to the fact that He is God. You may never have really honoured Him as God; He who has a claim upon you, He whose place is the throne of your heart.

"Now, give Him a reception, a royal reception. Honour Him and get down in the dust before Him; open the door of every chamber of your being; bring the keys of every department of your life, put them into His hands, and do not reserve anything. Oh, how often you have brought all, except one or two. You say, 'Ah, but that is such a little chamber. It is only a little drawer, I want to keep back that key.' You have never really then, given Him the reception that is due to Him. He is your Proprietor; you are His property, and He wants to come and live in His home. You are His home, and He wants to walk through every part of your being, to possess you, rule you, satisfy you, and use you. Believe, I say, to receive and let Him have His rightful place."

The Rev. Evan Hopkins then explained that this experience is not another blessing from God for a short-term reviving, but an indwelling of man by God – a welcomed invasion of our bodies by the Spirit. "When the answer comes," he preached, "you will find that it is not so much an outpouring, as an infilling, a welling up of the fountain within you. You had the Spirit before, if you are a believer. But now He fills you."

Rees Howells' eyes were opened when he listened to this man. He realised that the Holy Spirit is a Person, with all the faculties of a Person, exactly like the Saviour. The Spirit has a will, intelligence, emotions and a personality of His own. But Rees also understood that if the Holy Spirit was going to live His life in and through him, he must be given full rights to His new vessel. Rees said, "It never dawned on me before that the Holy Spirit is a Person exactly like Christ, and that He must come and dwell in flesh and blood. I had only thought of Him as an Divine influence coming on meetings, and that was what most of us in the Welsh Revival thought."

The Bible reveals the Holy Spirit is the Third Person of the Trinity, and He is equal with the Father and the Son, in His Person and authority. He is One with the Father and the Son. In Matthew 10:20 the Son called the Holy Spirit, "The Spirit of your Father." However, as Rees Howells learnt, the Holy Spirit does not have a body to dwell in, and He seeks out the bodies of believers to live and abide in (1 Corinthians 3:17, 6:19). The Spirit is always given to those who ask God (Luke 11:13), and if we lack His Presence it is because we are lacking in obedience (Acts 5:32).

In the Bible, the Holy Spirit is called God (1 Corinthians 12:4-6, 2 Corinthians 3:17), and Peter said, "Ananias, why has Satan filled your heart to lie to the Holy Spirit...you have not lied to men but to God" (Acts 5:3-4). When Jesus commanded His followers to make disciples of all nations He told them to baptise, "In the name of the Father and of the Son and of the Holy Spirit" (Matthew 28:18-19). All three Persons are honoured together. The Spirit is omnipresent and He is One with the Lord: 'Where can I go from Your Spirit? Or where can I flee from Your presence?' (Psalm 139:7).

In the Old Testament, God the Father was often called Lord, and in the Church we call Jesus Lord, but do we know that the Bible states the Holy Spirit is Lord too? (2 Corinthians 3:17). The Father is Lord, the Son is Lord and Spirit is Lord. Jesus is Lord over the Church and the Holy Spirit should be exercising Christ's Lordship in our bodies – His temples (1 Corinthians 6:19). The Church can only be effective when it depends on the Spirit to manifest the Lordship of Christ in its members – us!

These Trinitarian principles in the Church are also found in 1 Corinthians 12:4-6. 'There are different kinds of gifts, but the same Spirit distributes them. There are different kinds of service, but the same Lord. There are different kinds of working, but in all of them and in everyone it is the same God at work.' We have the Spirit, v4, the Lord, v5, and God the Father, v6.

The Holy Spirit, like God the Father and God the Son, has always existed – He is 'the eternal Spirit' (Hebrews 9:14). The Spirit is also the Creator who 'was hovering over the face of the waters' (Genesis 1:2). God the Father was speaking with the Son and the Holy Spirit when He said, "Let Us make man in Our image" (Genesis 1:26, Colossians 1:16-18).

The Holy Spirit has an intellect and He reveals the deep things of God: 'God has revealed them to us through His Spirit. For the Spirit searches all things, yes, the deep things of God...no one knows the things of God except the Spirit of God' (1 Corinthians 2:10-11).

Some believe they can have access to God without the Spirit. But what does the Bible say? 'For through Him (Christ) we both have access by one Spirit to the Father' (Ephesians 2:18). Therefore, through the Son, by the Spirit, is the route to the Father. If we remove the Spirit from our lives and churches, there is no access to God!

Jesus and the Father are One (John 10:30-33), and the Spirit of God is the Spirit of Christ (1 Peter 1:11). Thus any church without the Spirit is akin to a well without water (John 4:13-14), due to the fact that one of the purposes of any church is to be a dwelling place of the Holy Spirit: 'In whom you also are being built together for a dwelling place of God in the Spirit' (Ephesians 2:22). If churches are to make a home fit for the Spirit, why do many know so little of Him?

The principle of the Trinity working in unity in the Church is found again in Ephesians. 'There is one body (the Church), and one *Spirit*, just as you were called to one hope when you were called; one *Lord*, one faith, one baptism; one *God and Father* of all, who is over all and through all and in all' (Ephesians 4:4-6). In this passage we have – one Spirit, one Lord and one God – all working together to get the message of the gospel to the world!

The Holy Spirit is a Person and He must be given His right to speak and guide the Church. The early Christians were sensitive to the will of the Holy Spirit: 'They were forbidden by the Holy Spirit to preach the Word in Asia…the Spirit did not permit them' (Acts 16:6-7). They were sensitive to His thoughts: He 'knows what the mind of the Spirit is' (Romans 8:27). They also allowed the Spirit to live and work through them, as Jesus said, "The wind blows where it wishes, and you hear the sound of it, but cannot tell where it comes from and where it goes. So is everyone born of the Spirit" (John 3:8)

The Spirit can be resisted, rejected and grieved, and Christians are warned: 'Do not grieve the Holy Spirit' (Ephesians 4:30), and the religious people were told: 'You always resist the Holy Spirit; as your father's did' (Acts 7:51).

The Holy Spirit will not come to abide in dirty vessels or live in a complacent church (Isaiah 52:11), because we must 'be holy because God is holy' (1 Peter 1:16). In recent years, it has become fashionable for Christians to seek a new anointing, or greater blessing by travelling to a place where the Holy Spirit is moving. It is biblical to receive a blessing from one who has already walked further with the Lord; however, those who follow in the footsteps of a powerful man or woman of God, still have to pay the same price as he or she did to walk in a similar anointing. There are no drive-through breakthroughs to become sensitive to the Spirit of God.

The young man Elisha, who received the mantle from Elijah, could not avoid full surrender, paying the price and embracing the cross. It was only when Elisha had sacrificed everything that his pathway of Holy Spirit discipleship began (1 Kings 19:21). Then he spent many years as Elijah's servant, carrying out the most humbling tasks anyone could do in his culture (Mark 10:42-45).

The great danger today is that many believers want the power of the Holy Spirit, but not the Person. Samuel Rees Howells (1912-2004), the son and successor of Rees Howells, was very concerned that people wanted to be blessed by the Holy Spirit, but not possessed by Him. Paul describes what it means to be possessed by the Holy Spirit when he wrote concerning being 'filled with the fullness of God' (Ephesians 3:19). This is more than a blessing, but being consumed and filled to the depths with the Spirit. How many want to feel His presence touching them, but not consuming them? This is a danger for us all. The baptism of fire is an ongoing all consuming relationship with the Holy Spirit. He burns away the chaff in our lives and fills us with His power for service.

We may chase a new blessing, but what we really need is the Blesser. We may seek a new anointing, but our deepest need is to meet the Person of the Holy Spirit in all His fullness. How much of ourselves have we given to the Holy Spirit to use for the glorification of Jesus Christ? Have we opened every area of our hearts, minds and spirits to the Holy Spirit? Are we His vessels or do we hold much back from Him? The Scriptures declare: 'You shall love the Lord your God with all your heart, with all your soul, and with all your strength' (Deuteronomy 6:5).

As a young evangelist, Oswald J. Smith in 1913 penned in his diary: 'I am determined that God shall have all there is of Oswald J. Smith.' In September he wrote and signed a threefold declaration: 'I will think no thought, speak no word, and do no deed unworthy of a follower of Jesus Christ. I give my life for service in any part of the world, and in any capacity God wills that I should labour. I shall endeavour to do God's will from moment to moment, as He reveals it to me.'[2]

Who is the Holy Spirit? In the Bible the Spirit of God reveals at least twenty-five names He can be known by and each name unveils more of who He is. Here are some of them:

• The Spirit of the Lord, Wisdom and Understanding, Counsel and Might, Knowledge and Fear of the Lord (Isaiah 11:2).
• The Spirit of Truth (John 14:17).
• The Comforter (John 14:26).
• The Spirit of Holiness (Romans 1:4).
• The Spirit of Life (Romans 8:2).
• The Spirit of Christ (Romans 8:9).
• The Spirit of Adoption (Romans 8:15).
• The Eternal Spirit (Hebrews 9:14).
• The Spirit of Grace (Hebrews 10:29).
• The Spirit of Glory (1 Peter 4:14).

Christians have often struggled with the question of their relationship with the Trinity. Should we honour the Father and the Son together, and what of the Spirit? Our finite minds struggle to understand this, but when we listen to and obey the Spirit, we are listening to and obeying the Father and Son – they are One.

In the Church we often speak of Jesus being in our midst, but truly it is the Holy Spirit who is with us, as He manifests the Lord's Presence amongst us and urges us to be conformed to the image of

Christ (Romans 8:29). Jesus is literally in heaven (1 Thessalonians 1:10, Acts 3:21, Hebrews 1:3, 12:2), but He is with us in the Person of the Spirit (Matthew 18:20), and when the Spirit transforms us into the image of Christ, we become closer to the image of the Father. Therefore, when we reject the Holy Spirit, we are equally rejecting the Father and the Son (1 John 2:23); but if we want to receive the Father and the Son, we must also receive the Holy Spirit in all His fullness (Matthew 11:27, Luke 10:22, John 5:19-26, 8:28, 14:13).

The Holy Spirit is God on earth. He is so important to the fulfilment of the Lord's plans that He receives a special protection and we are warned not to decry Him. Jesus said, "Therefore I say to you, every sin and blasphemy will be forgiven men, but the blasphemy against the Spirit will not be forgiven men. Anyone who speaks a word against the Son of Man, it will be forgiven him; but whoever speaks against the Holy Spirit, it will not be forgiven him, either in this age or in the age to come" (Matthew 12:31-32). Why does God need to give this special warning to mankind? Because it is the Holy Spirit who will complete the work of God on earth, through the vessels He finds. If we reject Him, the work cannot be completed.

Some Christians are concerned that they may have committed the unpardonable sin in ignorance, but William P. Nicholson writing in the 1940s, brings comfort to those who believe they are guilty: 'The unpardonable sin is the continued and obstinate rejection of Christ until there comes a time when His Spirit ceases to strive, and the offer of mercy and forgiveness is withdrawn, and you are left to your doom and damnation.'[3] He continued: 'Don't let Satan tell you, you are doomed because you have committed the unpardonable sin. He is a liar and the father of lies. The very fact of your deep distress and miserable feeling is the surest sign you have not committed the sin. He is a liar. Any and every reason you may give that helps you delay believing in Christ is of the devil and for your damnation. If Christ was not willing to save you, He wouldn't have awakened you and made you miserable about your sins.'[4] The apostle Paul was once a blasphemer, but he testified: 'I obtained mercy because I did it ignorantly in unbelief' (1 Timothy 1:13).

*Questions to consider:* Do you know the Person of the Holy Spirit? Have you perceived Him as God?
*Actions:* Ask the Lord Jesus to give you a revelation of the Holy Spirit and follow Him wherever He leads.

# Chapter Ten

## The Trinity in Unity

- 'In the beginning *God* created the heavens and the earth. The earth was without form and void; and darkness was on the face of the deep. And the *Spirit of God* was hovering over the face of the waters' (Genesis 1:1-2). See John 1:3 and Colossians 1:16-17.
- "Let Us make man in Our image" (Genesis 1:26).
- "The *Lord God* and His *Spirit* have sent *Me*" (Isaiah 48:16).
- 'Until the day in which *He (Christ)* was taken up, after He through the *Holy Spirit* had given commandments to the apostles whom He had chosen' (Acts 1:2).
- Peter said to them, "Repent, and let every one of you be baptised in the name of *Jesus Christ* for the remission of sins and you shall receive the gift of the *Holy Spirit*. For the promise is to you and to your children, and to all who are afar off, as many as the *Lord our God* will call" (Acts 2:36-39).
- 'For through *Him (Christ)*, we both have access to the *Father* by one *Spirit*' (Ephesians 2:18).
- 'There is one body and *one Spirit*, just as you were called to one hope when you were called; *one Lord*, one faith, one baptism; one *God and Father* of all, who is over all and through all and in all' (Ephesians 4:4-6).
- 'How much more shall the blood of *Christ (the Son)*, who through the eternal *Spirit (the Holy Spirit)* offered Himself without spot to *God (the Father)*, cleanse your conscience from dead works to serve the living God?' (Hebrews 9:14).
- 'Of how much worse punishment, do you suppose, will he be thought worthy who has trampled the *Son of God* underfoot *(Son and Father)*, counted the blood of the covenant by which he was sanctified a common thing, and insulted the *Spirit of grace (The Holy Spirit)*?' (Hebrews 10:29).
- 'The *Spirit of Christ* who was in them was indicating when He testified beforehand the sufferings of *Christ*' (1 Peter 1:11).
- 'If you are reproached for the name of *Christ*, blessed are you, for the *Spirit of glory* and of *God* rests upon you. On their part He is blasphemed, but on your part He is glorified' (1 Peter 4:14).
- 'This is the One who came by water and blood – *Jesus Christ*. He did not come by water only, but by water and blood. And it is the *Spirit* who testifies, because the *Spirit* is the Truth' (1 John 5:6).

# Chapter Eleven

## The Voice and Leading of the Spirit

Some have been taught that the baptism of the Holy Spirit is the final experience we can receive from God. However, the experiences we have with the Holy Spirit will always be measured by our willingness to let go, and allow Him to fill us. If we only allow Him to touch small areas of our lives, His ability to change us will also be small. It is not that He is restricted, but that we have restricted Him. As we limit God's ability to live in us, He is limited in His ability to bless us and transform our lives to make us more like Christ. This is why many people who have received the baptism of the Holy Spirit and were blessed, have now stagnated in their faith. We all need the baptism of fire in the Holy Spirit.

Evangelist and revivalist Gipsy Smith said in the 1920s, "Thou shalt have no other gods before Me. He must have the place of the throne in your heart and in your home. He will not share your devotion with another. He is a jealous God. He gave you everything in life worth having and He demands from you your best in return. Nothing else will satisfy Him. He demands a whole surrender."[1]

"I have learnt something as the Spirit of God has led me," said a disciple of the Lord. "If I live my life seeking what I feel, want or think I desire, it always leads to spiritual death (Romans 8:7, Galatians 5:16-18). But when I follow the leading of the Spirit, my flesh life dies and my spirit overcomes the flesh (Matthew 16:25). The more my flesh dies, the more the life of Christ is revealed in me (1 John 2:16). As this took place in my life, I learnt to be led by the Spirit of God and this is the proof that I am a child of God. Imagine therefore my surprise when I was reading the Bible and it explained what was happening to me! 'For if you live according to the flesh, you will die; but if by the Spirit you put to death the misdeeds of the body, you will live. For those who are led by the Spirit of God are the children of God' " (Romans 8:14-15).

The Holy Spirit desires to make what we call 'Christians' into disciples of the Lord Jesus Christ. To do this, He will begin to speak to us about areas in our lives that do not please Him (Colossians 3:5-10). The Holy Spirit leads us into holiness because He wants to take ground in our lives that belongs to the enemy and claim it for Christ. He comes to possess the land which was once possessed by the flesh, the world and the devil. He comes, like Joshua, to redeem the land in our lives and expel the invaders who currently possess His possession (Exodus 23:30, Joshua 13:1, 18:3).

The process of allowing the Holy Spirit to change our lives is the beginning of God's purpose to renew our minds (Romans 12:1-2).

When we were saved, our minds were not renewed to think like God wants us to think, because it is a process which we are commanded to undertake ourselves. This is why many believers still think like the world, they still live according to the will of the flesh and their carnal natures still leans towards fulfilling the will of the Kingdom of darkness (John 8:44, Romans 8:13, Colossians 3:5-7).

One of the greatest problems in the Church is that Christian people have never had their minds renewed to view the world from a biblical perspective (Ephesians 4:23). For this reason, when they are faced with a biblical truth, instead of accepting it, they filter it out and dilute it by the measure of current culture and its worldview. The Holy Spirit will speak to us and show us that our minds have been contaminated by the deception of this world and only He, with the living Word, can change our understanding of everything!

In His light, we learn that our entire view of what is right and wrong, what is truth and a lie has been perverted by the world (Isaiah 5:20), and the Holy Spirit wants to transform our thinking and worldview. The Holy Spirit will use the Bible to calibrate our knowledge of truth and error, and transform our beliefs about what is correct and amiss. John explains this experience: 'But the anointing which you have received from Him abides in you, and you do not need that anyone teach you; but as the same anointing teaches you concerning all things, and is true, and is not a lie, and just as it has taught you, you will abide in Him' (1 John 2:27).

Our culture has corrupted our minds and we have believed evil to be good and good evil (Isaiah 5:20). But we need to allow the Holy Spirit to change our ways of thinking, so that we can perceive reality in the way that God sees it. When we were first converted our worldly natures may not have believed in demons, angels, blessings and curses, but through the Bible and our experiences, the Holy Spirit will open our eyes to the reality of this life and the next.

When we were young Christians, we may have thought that tithing was man's way of taking money from religious people, but now the Holy Spirit reveals it is His will for us to be His channel to bless the world by sowing and reaping (2 Corinthians 9:6, Galatians 6:7). The flesh, or carnal nature will resist all the change which the Holy Spirit is trying to bring into our lives and our response to the flesh should not be to pacify its will, but to crucify it, as Jesus demands (Matthew 16:24, Romans 6:6).

Once we may have believed in a culture of 'rights,' but the Spirit will show us that we have no rights when we have placed our lives on God's altar. The Spirit will lead us to change our 'cultural or national worldview' to a biblical worldview. The question will not be, what does my culture believe about this subject, but what does the Bible say? (2 Timothy 3:16).

However, we may ask: How can I learn to be sensitive to the voice and leading of the Holy Spirit? Learning to discern His voice begins when we choose to become sensitive to the inner grieving of the Spirit in our spirit. Jesus gave us this promise, "My sheep hear My voice" (John 10:27). As this is the case, we should all expect Him to speak to us, but we must learn to *listen* to what He is saying and how He speaks. Jesus also explained that the Spirit of Truth will guide us into all truth and, "He will tell you things to come...He will take what is Mine and declare it to you" (John 16:13-15).

When we are engaged in activities which are contrary to the purposes of Christ in our lives, the Holy Spirit within us will grieve (Ephesians 4:30). We will spiritually discern His displeasure and we may physically feel His conviction within our bodies and spirits. Jesus said, "He who believes in Me as the Scriptures has said out of his belly shall flow rivers of living water" (John 7:38).

Many believers have found that the belly area of the body appears to be where the physical and spiritual part of our being coincides. When the Holy Spirit is praying through us, we often sense the overflow of His prayer from within our belly area. When the Holy Spirit comes upon someone, sometimes a physical manifestation explodes from the belly area and out to the rest of the body. With this in mind, we learn to sense the Spirit grieving, as we tune our spiritual ears towards the part of us that is spiritual. As we begin to obey the 'inner witness' of the Holy Spirit, this will prepare us to hear His voice.

"I had experienced some powerful encounters with the Holy Spirit," said a disciple of the Lord. "But after a few days the peace that flooded my soul and His Presence diminished. I asked the Lord why I was experiencing this and He showed me I was spending a great deal of time judging other Christians (James 4:11-12). The Holy Spirit revealed that I cannot have the peace of God and allow my mind to be judgmental, critical and negative" (Matthew 7:1).

Many hope to hear God speaking to them in an audible voice, but most disciples of Jesus hear the Holy Spirit as He speaks to them in the inner man. They have an idea, thought, question, Scripture or leading placed within their spirit or mind. Then, they must respond to it. As an example, the Holy Spirit may say, "Go to...," and in this context the Scripture is being fulfilled: 'Your ears shall hear a Word behind you saying, "This is the way, walk in it" ' (Isaiah 30:21).

Hearing God is often only possible when we choose to spend time with God, and quieten the noise of the world. If we are busy thinking about politics, the news, or have songs playing in our minds, we may not be able to hear or discern properly because our spirits are overwhelmed with the distractions and noise (Psalm 46:10, Isaiah

40:31). But when we continue in fellowship and daily communion with God in prayer, and learn to abide in God's presence at all times, we will gradually become more sensitive to His voice – *if* we obey (James 1:22, John 14:15, 14:21, 1 John 5:2). Paul wrote about this, calling it "the fellowship of the Spirit" (Philippians 2:1).

"Many years ago I was looking at a map and the Holy Spirit made a name of a village stick out," said a disciple of the Lord. "I knew the Lord wanted me to go there and when I arrived, I saw a man working in a field and was prompted to talk to him. As I spoke with him, I discovered he had been banned from his very religious pharisaical church, but he still wanted to be in right relation to God. So I told him, 'You must be born again!' The man responded, "That's what I want!" I led him to the Lord that day and I was amazed at the lengths the Holy Spirit is prepared to go to save one soul! Like Philip, I was led directly to him" (Acts 8:26-32).

When the Holy Spirit speaks to us and asks us for an act of obedience, this can often be a stepping stone for us to take a leap of faith. Then, when we have moved out into the unknown, the Spirit will guide us to the next step. In this way, we receive a progressive revelation of His will and purposes.

"The Spirit revealed to me that I had to go back and put right the things I had done wrong in the past," said a disciple of the Lord. "The Bible states we shall reap what we sow, and the Spirit told me to go back to confess, repent, apologise and make restitutions for my past sins (Leviticus 5:5, Proverbs 28:13, Ecclesiastes 3:15, Luke 19:8, Ephesians 4:28). It was a humbling experience, but I was sowing the seed of obedience and later I reaped the blessings of obedience."

These examples indicate how very important it is for us to learn to become sensitive to the voice and leading of the Holy Spirit. It is He who reveals the truth and gives us the keys to our breakthroughs. We must learn to discern between His voice and others, and we must be aware that the Spirit of God will only continue to speak to us, with the same measure we listen in obedience to Him. If we never obey the Holy Spirit, He will stop speaking to us! If we obey Him, He will know that we are serious and He will return to us again and again!

'The surrendered life means the common everyday life, sanctified,' wrote Gideon L. Powell, 'Not my will but Thine' is the prayer of his heart, and his life is made to harmonise with the will of God.'[2] Listening to and obeying the Holy Spirit means harmonising our lives with His perfect will.

*Questions to consider:* Do you want the Holy Spirit to lead you? Do you want to become sensitive to the voice of the Holy Spirit?
*Actions:* Make up your mind to obey the Spirit, whatever He asks.

# Chapter Twelve

## Acts of the Holy Spirit

### Baptised and Witnessed by the Holy Spirit

- 'For with stammering lips and another tongue He will speak to this people' (Isaiah 28:11).
- 'They were all filled with the Holy Spirit and began to speak with other tongues, as the Spirit gave them utterance' (Acts 2:4).
- "Therefore let all the house of Israel know assuredly that God has made this Jesus, whom you crucified, both Lord and Christ." Now when they heard this, they were cut to the heart, and said to Peter and the rest of the apostles, "Men and brethren, what shall we do?" Then Peter said to them, "Repent, and let every one of you be baptised in the name of Jesus Christ for the remission of sins and you shall receive the gift of the Holy Spirit. For the promise is to you and to your children, and to all who are afar off, as many as the Lord our God will call" (Acts 2:36-39).
- 'Then Peter, filled with the Holy Spirit said to them, "Rulers of the people and elders of Israel" ' (Acts 4:8).
- 'When they had prayed, the place where they were assembled together was shaken; and they were all filled with the Holy Spirit, and they spoke the Word of God with boldness…and with great power the apostles gave witness to the resurrection of the Lord Jesus, and great grace was upon them all' (Acts 4:31, 33).
- 'Stephen, being full of the Holy Spirit, gazed into heaven and saw the glory of God, and Jesus standing at the right hand of God' (Acts 5:55).
- 'Stephen, full of faith and power, did great wonders and signs among the people' (Acts 6:8).
- 'Who, when they had come down, prayed for them that they might receive the Holy Spirit' (Acts 8:15).
- 'Ananias went his way and entered the house and laying his hands on him he said, "Brother Saul, the Lord Jesus, who appeared to you on the road as you came, has sent me that you may receive your sight and be filled with the Holy Spirit" ' (Acts 9:17).
- 'That we might receive the promise of the Spirit through faith' (Galatians 3:14).

# Chapter Thirteen

## Discerning His Voice

In the Old Testament, men and women of God had limited ways to hear from God, but for believers in Christ, we have God Himself living on the inside. He is our Teacher and Guide (John 16:13). We do not have to seek Him in a far off place, or go on a trip to Jerusalem to find Him; He lives in us and we in Him (1 Corinthians 6:19). Therefore, becoming sensitive to His voice and leadings, and being able to distinguish between Him and other voices is essential.

When we seek to obey the Holy Spirit, Satan may try to use our newfound desire for righteousness as a tool to chastise us (2 Corinthians 11:14). One young person believed God told him that any rubbish on the street was sin; therefore he had to pick up every piece of rubbish! This person spent the next few months picking up rubbish everywhere and through a demonic leading, Satan destroyed the individual's desire to obey God and live righteously. It wasn't the Holy Spirit who was leading him, but Satan who was chastising him and abusing his desire to follow God.

Jesus said, "He who does not enter the sheepfold by the door, but climbs up some other way, the same is a thief and a robber. But he who enters by the door is the shepherd of the sheep. To him the doorkeeper opens, and the sheep hear his voice; and he calls his own sheep by name and leads them out...the sheep follow him, for they know his voice...My sheep hear My voice, and I know them, and they follow Me and I give them eternal life..." (John 10:1-4, 27-28). We therefore have a promise from Jesus that we should hear His voice, by the power and Person of the Holy Spirit.

God has promised to guide the believer, but we must bear in mind that there are conditions that must be met (Psalm 25:9, 32:8, Isaiah 42:6). It is self-defeating to believe that God will reveal things to us, when we are in deliberate, obstinate, wilful sin, which we refuse to confront (Psalm 66:18, Proverbs 28:9, Isaiah 59:2-15, Ezekiel 14:3). Equally true, we cannot expect God to reveal His 'personal will' to us, if we have not obeyed the 'revealed will' of God, as found in the Holy Bible. We do not need to pray to find out if forgiving is right, or if stealing is wrong because God has already told us His will. Additionally, we cannot expect God to give us personal revelations of His will, if we have not obeyed the last thing He told us to do!

"The leading of the Spirit is such a sensitive area," said a disciple of the Lord. "I have met people in full-time Christian ministry who are lost and deceived, because they belittled direct commands from the

Holy Spirit and they did not obey. If we deliberately ignore a sure Word from the Holy Spirit, or if we treat it as 'nothing,' we will find ourselves like Jonah in dangerous waters (Proverbs 29:1).

God always speaks for very important reasons and to casually dismiss His command is a great sin. This is why the Bible warns: 'Do not quench the Spirit. Do not despise prophecies,' and then it adds the importance of discerning His voice: 'Test all things; hold fast what is good' (1 Thessalonians 5:19-21).

It is possible for us all to get very busy for God, but never actually be serving Him. Paul warned our 'good works' will be burnt in the judgment, if they were not directed by God (1 Corinthians 3:9-17).

"I have been concerned that Christians are often looking for 'the latest thing' or are busy 'networking' in the flesh searching for 'new campaigns and projects' that sweep the Christian world," said a disciple of the Lord. "Why are they so quick to jump on the latest bandwagon? Having zeal is great, but wouldn't it be better to give all to the Lord and learn to become sensitive to the Holy Spirit? He has a ministry for them – why follow man?" (Ephesians 2:10).

Some people preach that 'the need constitutes a call.' Yet this is contrary to the teaching of Jesus (Luke 4:25-27, Mark 14:7). It is the Holy Spirit who reveals God's will and it is He who calls, sends forth and forbids. The Bible states: 'They were forbidden by the Holy Spirit to preach the Word in Asia. After they had come to Mysia, they tried to go into Bithynia, but the Spirit did not permit them' (Acts 16:6-7). Therefore, the Holy Spirit may forbid us to do something good because it is not our call, or the right time.

"I knew a Christian man who really wanted to be used by God," said a disciple of the Lord. "Outwardly he knew the Bible, could preach, teach and was a good person. However, there were major areas of his life which he refused to submit to Jesus. He refused to walk in the revealed will of God in the Bible, because he would not tithe etc. This outward disobedience was a sign of His inward battle with God – he was resisting God and would not surrender all to Him. The Lord tried to reach out to him many times and every time he said, 'I don't believe in tithing,' etc., and he always had excuses.

"He may not realise it, but because he refused to obey the revealed will of God, he disqualified himself from receiving the direct and personal leading of the Holy Spirit. In truth, he refused to hear what the Spirit was trying to teach him. Finally, because he refused to heed what the Holy Spirit had to say to him, another spirit took advantage and came as an angel of light (2 Corinthians 11:14). Suddenly 'god' had spoken to him about a ministry opportunity which he followed and it ended in dismal failure. He blamed God for this failure and was never willing to have his eyes opened to the real truth. What lesson did I learn from this? If we refuse to obey God's revealed will, and refuse to heed His conviction and repent – we open ourselves up to deception (James 1:22). The very act of disobeying God is the first step into a life of deception – because we are deliberately rejecting the truth and embracing a lie. One of the judgments of God is to allow people to live under the shadow of their own deception. As people refuse God's will for them He 'gives them up to' or 'gives them over to' their foolishness and sin (Acts 7:42, Romans 1:24, 26). People are often chastised by the results of their own sin (Matthew 15:13-14). What should our response be? Repent first. Get right with God and obey His Word. Respond to His conviction and then He will speak to us about other things!"

**How God Can Speak to Us**
- Through the Scriptures, His Word the Holy Bible.
- The inner witness and refined conscience (Acts 15:28, 1 John 3:20-21).
- The Holy Spirit's small still voice (1 Kings 19:9-18, John 14:26, Acts 10:19, 13:2, Romans 8:16).
- Being rebuked by others, even non-believers – "Christians shouldn't do that!"
- Through Christians – by the exercising of the gifts of the Holy Spirit: a word of wisdom, knowledge or a prophecy (Jeremiah 42, 1 Corinthians 12-14). But if we receive a word via another believer, we must weigh it and pray it. Test the spirits whether they are of God or not (1 Thessalonians 5:19-21, 1 John 4:1-3). If you are not sure then ask God for confirmation (1 Corinthians 14:26, 2 Corinthians 13:1).
- God can speak through nature or by inanimate objects, e.g. a book, the television, a magazine, etc., something just sticks out or jumps out and grabs your attention.
- By a dream, vision or trance (Genesis 41:8, 15-16, Acts 10:16).
- Audibly, though this is not common (Exodus 3:4, 33:11).

Discerning the voice of God comes through experience, but even mature Christians make mistakes and may get a direction wrong, or interpret it incorrectly. Often when we give or receive a prophetic word – it can be like a coin – two-sided in nature; therefore we must make sure we look at the right side! Reading too much into a prophetic word – going beyond the revelation, or adding to it, will lead to big problems. What exactly did God say?

With this in mind, if the word you believe you have received from God will lead to a major life changing experience, then it is wise to ask another on fire, well proven and tested prophetic believer. Don't ask your backslidden friend, or an elder who has lost his first love, because he can't help you! John explained that the first century Christian leader Diotrephes was outside of God's will and he even put people out of the church for listening to the teaching of the apostles! (3 John 9-10). If such leaders can't hear from God, how can they help others hear from Him?

However, if you have received a word to make a small personal sacrifice, perhaps to give some money to a poor person and witness, then go ahead! We can afford to make small sacrifices by mistake, but we can't afford to get life changing directions wrong.

The Bible is the greatest guide to help us discern the will of the Lord. God will never tell us to do anything that contradicts His Word as revealed in the Holy Bible. The Lord will never ask us to commit sin, act selfishly or deceive. We must know that any direction we receive can be from God, the devil, or from one's own imagination – wishful thinking (Jeremiah 14:14, 23:25-36). But how can we tell the difference between them?

The Holy Spirit speaks lovingly, reassuringly and encouragingly. Out of love He may rebuke us and this will lead us to repentance (Hebrews 12:5). God's direction fulfilled in our lives will bring peace, even if He rebukes us (Colossians 3:15). Whereas the devil accuses, nags and speaks in a mocking manner. The enemy will try to confuse us by sowing doubt, fear and discouragement into our minds, "Did God really say?" (Genesis 3:1-4).

"One thing I have learnt is that the Holy Spirit is never in a hurry," said a disciple of the Lord. "There may be a few 'suddenly' events in our lives where we have to step out in faith; but in general, the Holy Spirit speaks to us, giving us plenty of time and deals with us over long periods. He does not need to rush us into an act of obedience, because He has all the time in the world. He represents the Alpha and the Omega, and one day with Him is like a thousand years (2 Peter 3:8). He spent forty years preparing Moses in the wilderness; forty seconds won't be enough for us. If we rush and hurry, we may step ahead of God, and the enemy can mislead us when we are in a hurry. Also, God does not speak to us daily with new directions and plans. His plan is unfolded over years of faith and patience."

We may sometimes seek God for a sign, but this should be a rare occurrence because the Spirit is the One who leads us into all truth. In the Old Testament, it was only the chosen few who received the Holy Spirit, therefore most of the others relied on signs (Judges 6:37-40), or sought spiritual leaders who used the Urim and the Thummim to seek God. Nobody knows exactly what the Urim and the Thummim were, but possibly they were like lots (Proverbs 16:33). The kings of Israel and other people asked the High Priest to enquire of God via the Urim and Thummim on their behalf (1 Samuel 28:6, Ezra 2:63 and Nehemiah 7:65).

In the New Testament, believers in Christ do not need to rely on signs or seek the lots of the Old Testament, because we have been given the Spirit to guide us and direct us into all truth (John 16:13).

Therefore, our focus must be on learning to become sensitive to His voice and leading. 'Increasingly guidance is felt,' wrote John White, 'not in the strange and miraculous, but continuously in a developing sensitivity to an abiding relationship.'[1]

It is this abiding relationship which we must seek with the Spirit, until we become sensitive to His still small voice. Becoming truly sensitive to His voice will take years and even decades, but the more we walk with Him in obedience, the more we receive from Him. Nevertheless, the principle of obedience leading to sensitivity still stands! If you obey the Holy Spirit when He speaks, you give Him a reason to speak to you again!

The original source of the following guide, with amendments, is unknown, but the wisdom within remains very useful in our quest.

## The Holy Spirit or the Condemnation of Satan?
• The Holy Spirit is gentle and loving. Satan condemns.
• The Spirit gives encouragement. Satan brings discouragement.
• The Holy Spirit disciplines us in love. Satan tries to destroy us.
• The Holy Spirit convicts us of sin. Satan encourages us to sin.
• The Spirit points us to God. Satan wants us to run from God.
• The Spirit confirms confessed sin is forgiven. Satan says, "Not!"
• The Spirit reminds us there is hope. Satan tells us there is none.
• The Spirit points us to the Bible. Satan points us to our feelings.
• The Spirit reminds us of the cross. Satan reminds us of comfort.
• The Spirit leads us to forget self. Satan leads us to nourish self.
• The Spirit guides us to crucifixion. Satan encourages the flesh.
• The Spirit tells us to forgive. Satan urges us to keep an offence.
• The Spirit urges us to be better. Satan wants us to be selfish.
• The Spirit wants true fellowship. Satan wants troubled isolation.
• The Spirit reminds us who we are in Christ. Satan highlights our weakness and failings, stating God would never use us.
• The Holy Spirit reassures us of God's love. Satan accuses and says we're hated and rejected.

*Questions to consider:* Are you learning to distinguish between the Holy Spirit, the flesh and the demonic counterfeit? Are you asking God to give you wisdom and the gift of discernment? (James 1:5).
*Actions:* Test the spirits and see if they are from God.

# Chapter Fourteen

## Qualifications for Service

- 'He said to them, "Did you receive the Holy Spirit when you believed?" So they said to him, "We have not so much as heard whether there is a Holy Spirit." When they heard this, they were baptised in the name of the Lord Jesus. And when Paul had laid hands on them, the Holy Spirit came upon them, and they spoke with tongues and prophesied' (Acts 19:2, 5-6).
- "We are His witnesses to these things and so also is the Holy Spirit whom God has given to those who obey Him" (Acts 5:32).
- 'Therefore, brethren, seek out from among you seven men of good reputation, full of the Holy Spirit and wisdom, whom we may appoint over this business…and they chose Stephen, a man full of faith and power, who did great wonders and signs among the people…and they were not able to resist the wisdom and the Spirit by which he spoke' (Acts 6:3, 5, 8, 10).
- 'For he was a good man, full of the Holy Spirit and of faith, and a great many people were added to the Lord' (Acts 11:24).
- 'And the disciples were filled with joy and with the Holy Spirit' (Acts 13:52).
- 'Therefore take heed to yourselves and to all the flock, among which the Holy Spirit has made you overseers' (Acts 20:28).
- 'Not that we are sufficient of ourselves to think of anything as being from ourselves, but our sufficiency is from God, who also made us sufficient as ministers of the new covenant, not of the letter but of the Spirit; for the letter kills, but the Spirit gives life. But if the ministry of death, written and engraved on stones, was glorious, so that the children of Israel could not look steadily at the face of Moses because of the glory of his countenance, which glory was passing away, how will the ministry of the Spirit not be more glorious?' (2 Corinthians 3:5-8).
- 'We who serve God by His Spirit, who boast in Christ Jesus and who put no confidence in the flesh' (Philippians 3:3).
- 'For this is the will of God, your sanctification: that you should abstain from sexual immorality…for God did not call us to be impure, but to live a holy life. Therefore, anyone who rejects this instruction does not reject a human being but God, the very God who gives you His Holy Spirit' (1 Thessalonians 4:3, 7-8).

# Chapter Fifteen

## The Holy Spirit Our Teacher

Every disciple of the Lord Jesus should be enrolled in the school of the Holy Spirit (1 John 2:27). This is the school where God's Spirit is both Teacher and Guide, as He leads us in our daily lives. When we enter this school, we will be trained twenty-four hours a day, seven days a week, as the Spirit teaches us how to live the Bible.

The Holy Spirit showed Rees Howells that He did not want him to only read the Bible, but to live what he read by the Spirit. This is what James also taught. 'But be doers of the Word and not hearers only, deceiving yourselves' (James 1:22). To be enrolled in the school of the Spirit, every willing student must ask the Holy Spirit to be his or her Teacher. One way to apply to be enrolled in this school is to get down on our knees before the Lord, confess and forsake our sin, surrender our lives and ask the Spirit of God to teach us the Bible through the circumstances that He leads us into.

If we humble ourselves and allow the Spirit of God to be our Teacher, we will begin to get to know Him as Guide in every area of our lives. Romans 8 is one of the great chapters on the work and ministry of the Holy Spirit, as Paul explains the need for the Holy Spirit to be our Teacher in every situation in our lives: For liberty (v2), purpose (v5), strength (v10), healing (v11), victory over sin (v13), guidance (v14), release from fear to sonship (v15), to be heirs (vs16-18), for the hope of heaven (v23), in prayer and intercession (v26), and to know the will and mind of God (v27).

The Holy Spirit will also teach us in many other ways. He may openly forbid us (Acts 16:5-10, Acts 19:10). We may experience a lack of peace (Colossians 3:15), or a lack of opportunity as doors close or open (1 Corinthians 16:8-9, Colossians 4:3, Revelation 3:8). There may also be a lack of a direct 'rhema Word' from God, for that moment (Psalm 119:105, Isaiah 30:1-2, 21).

In the book of Acts we learn how the Holy Spirit led the apostles: 'The Holy Spirit said,' 'Showed by the Spirit,' and, 'The Spirit told me' etc., are common themes (Acts 8:29, 39, Acts 10:19, Acts 11:12, 28, Acts 13:2, Acts 16:6-7). This teaches us that the Spirit of the Lord may also give us specific directions and commands.

John was enrolled in the school of the Holy Spirit and he expected all followers of the Lord Jesus Christ to be enrolled too: 'But the anointing which you have received from Him abides in you, and you do not need that anyone teach you; but as the same anointing teaches you concerning all things, and is true, and is not a lie, and just as it has taught you, you will abide in Him' (1 John 2:27).

John was not suggesting we will never need a human teacher, because one of the five-fold roles of leadership in the Church is for Spirit-led teachers (Ephesians 4:11). Instead, he was explaining that we all need an intimate relationship with the Holy Spirit, who will reveal all we need to know for our personal walk with Jesus Christ, as we follow the teaching of Scripture and abide in the Lord.

"When I read the Bible as a young person, I felt there was a new rule in every verse and I could never live up to those standards," explained a disciple of the Lord. "But as the years passed, I realised that the Holy Spirit wanted to be my Teacher and He led me to focus on one specific area until I got the victory. Then He would highlight something else. 'Little by little' He led me into victory (Exodus 23:30). Then I realised that everything He asked me to do was for my own joy. When the Bible states we should dwell on what is good (Philippians 4:8), I learnt this commandment has been given to us to help guard our own peace of mind. When I dwell on the good, my mind is at peace and is open to the Holy Spirit's voice. But when I dwell on the negative, my mind is in turmoil and I can't hear Him clearly."

In the school of the Holy Spirit, God will reveal sin, expose self and give us personal keys to victory. The Holy Spirit will also expose the hypocrisy of our lives and prayers. Before the Lord can move us forward in Him, He has to make us confront our own sin and the hindrances we have to God working in our lives. The baptism of fire is ongoing. It is not just a one-off experience we pray for; we live in the fire and the fire of God burns up our old lives.

"When I invited the Holy Spirit into my life to exercise the Lordship of Jesus Christ, I came to realise He would not tolerate me living my life as I previously had," said a disciple of the Lord. "He spoke to me about forgiveness, my attitude, my self-will, my thoughts and the way I treated others. I did not change overnight; it was step by step, as Isaiah stated: 'For precept must be upon precept, precept upon precept, line upon line, line upon line, here a little, there a little' " (Isaiah 28:10).

Many people in the school of the Holy Spirit find that the Teacher will start purging their lives of old ways and sins. Unforgiveness is a huge barrier to God working in our lives and the Holy Spirit will always highlight Christ's teaching on the subject (Matthew 6:14).

We may be praying for many things, but the Holy Spirit will reveal to us that we cannot get any victory whilst withholding forgiveness. Jesus taught this very clearly, yet so often we need the Holy Spirit to bring these things to remembrance and make them real in our lives (John 14:26).

The person with an unforgiving heart is like an individual who drinks poison everyday, hoping to make his or her enemy sick! It is the Holy Spirit who reveals our sin and when He shines His light on these areas, we must respond in the affirmative and agree with Him, leading to repentance. Yet, how often Christians try to hide their sins and deceive themselves (James 1:26, 1 John 1:8).

"At the end of the meetings I take, people often ask for prayer," said a disciple of the Lord. "As is my custom, I always ask the Holy Spirit to guide me and He often gives me words of knowledge or wisdom. What I discovered from these times, is that many of the problems that Christians have are not related to some unknown mystical demonic force that stops blessing, but the common sins of unforgiveness, bitterness, anger, rebellion, or indifference to the Lord's will. I asked one person if she had forgiven everyone and she replied, 'Yes.' Then the Holy Spirit said, 'Ask her about her aunty.' When I asked her, she cried out, 'I'll never forgive her!'

"Through this experience and many others, the Holy Spirit taught me the reason many people do not receive what they are asking for, is because there are many hidden hindrances which God is ever seeing. It's not the sins that they want to overcome as they struggle to be holy (Romans 7:15-25), but the sins they refuse to overcome (2 Corinthians 4:2).

"Whenever people refuse to obey the revealed will of God they deceive themselves (James 1:22), and pull a spiritual canopy or umbrella over their lives which keeps God's blessing off of them. Through experiences like these, the Holy Spirit taught me that it is a waste of time praying for healing or deliverance for a person who is in open rebellion to the revealed will of God in the Bible. First, they must repent and forsake their sins."

Some may believe that a sensitive relationship with the Holy Spirit is only possible for 'great men and women of God.' But this concept is unbiblical. All great men and women of God were once unknown, and in every age, people have embraced the cross, given themselves to the Holy Spirit and obeyed Him at all costs to follow Jesus Christ, and then they became 'great.' Equally true there is a secret which the Church often forgets. The greatest people of faith are most probably unknown; secret intercessors, prayer warriors and prophets, carefully concealed behind the titles of housewife or retired, or those working in remote locations, etc.

On the flip side of believing this relationship is only possible for 'great' people, is the mistake of thinking that we can never do anything unless we are led by some 'feeling.' Some use this concept as an excuse never to do anything; but those who give themselves to the Holy Spirit will ultimately discover that He will lead them to give far more than the average believer, because He will exercise the rights of the Lordship of Jesus Christ, to give all He can through us to reach the world with the gospel. If we give ourselves entirely to Him, He will lead us into God's perfect will.

Some have taught that God only speaks through the Bible and by memorising Scripture they can find the will of God, without needing to know the Holy Spirit as their Teacher. God has revealed Himself to us in the Word, but we cannot confine God to the pages of a Book, because in that Word He told us that He would send the Spirit to us to be our Teacher!

It is possible to become very familiar with the Bible, but not familiar with the God of the Bible. If we are not careful we may replace our relationship with God, with a relationship with a Book. This is what happened to the religious leaders in Christ's day. "You search the Scriptures, for in them you think you have eternal life; and these are they that testify of Me, but you are not willing to come to Me that you may have life" (John 5:39-40).

"For over a decade I used daily readings from a ministry," said a disciple of the Lord. "Then the Spirit said to me, 'I don't want you to read these any more. I want you to read the Bible and I want to interpret the Scripture for you.' For years I had been blessed by learning from other Christians the truth of God's Word, but now the Holy Spirit wanted to interpret Scripture for me personally. Man has many good ideas of how to interpret the Bible and we all need to be familiar with the doctrines of evangelical Christianity. However, only the Holy Spirit knows how to lead and guide us to understand the Bible, as it applies to our circumstances."

"You cannot provide your own interpretation of Scripture," said the influential Bible teacher Derek Prince (1915-2003). "There is only One authorised Interpreter – the Holy Spirit. The longer I'm in the ministry, the more I see that we only know God's truth by revelation. You can read the Bible and you can know the Bible from heart, but you don't see anything until God reveals it. To receive revelation takes time. You have to be prepared to wait before God and to meditate on the Scriptures. Not to rush. Revelation takes time and it often comes when we least expect it."[1]

Jesus prayed, "I thank you Father, Lord of heaven and earth, that You have hidden these things from the wise and prudent, and have revealed them to babes" (Matthew 11:25). Here we find Jesus noting the importance of being childlike in our faith – humble, willing to learn and receive from God. He is the living Word (John 1:1).

It is possible to be a professor of theology and to have memorised the Bible, yet still have no intimate knowledge of God. There is a great danger in relying on education, rather than revelation. Education enables the mind to memorise Scripture, revelation enables the Holy Spirit to make us live the Bible.

Many people have been called by God into ministry, but instead of drawing close to the Holy Spirit and following Him, they go to men to get an education from them. They learn to repeat things that other men have once said, and teach from the revelation that others have received. This is the pathway to fruitless Christianity and ministry, because Jesus' principles of abiding in John 15 have been ignored. Being trained in the faith is a good thing, but trusting in that training, rather than the leading of the Spirit of God will lead to disaster. Paul explained that it was the Holy Spirit who led the apostles and they had no confidence in their own abilities: 'We who serve God by His Spirit, who boast in Christ Jesus and who put no confidence in the flesh' (Philippians 3:3).

In 1949, in the Hebrides, UK, the Holy Spirit revealed to two elderly sisters that the famous preacher Duncan Campbell would come to the islands and revival would break out! When they told the local minister, he tried to invite Campbell, but it was impossible for him to come, so the minister told them it was not possible. With that, the sisters rebuked the minister for his unbelief and told him that God never lies! The Holy Spirit spoke to Campbell himself and soon he was sat humbly before these elderly sisters. The minister had a solid education, but these two elderly women had received revelation from the Holy Spirit. Revival soon followed!

The Bible teaches that God needs humble childlike faith for Him to touch the world. Scholars and theologians will debate if God speaks today and if people can be healed, whilst those led by the Holy Spirit will be hearing from God and seeing the sick healed!

Paul was a highly educated man who became entirely dependant on the Holy Spirit for revelation. He wrote: 'For you see your calling brethren, that not many wise according to the flesh, not many mighty, not many noble are called. But God has chosen the foolish things of the world to put to shame the wise, and God has chosen the weak things of the world to put to shame the things which are mighty, and the base things of the world and the things which are despised God has chosen, and the things which are not, to bring to nothing the things that are, that no flesh should glory in His presence' (1 Corinthians 1:26-29).

Samuel Rees Howells said, "There is no satisfaction nor conviction in anything unless it has been given by a revelation, otherwise it is only mental assent," and, "Teaching will never change your position, words and phrases do not convey anything."[2] Samuel, as the director of a Bible College, wasn't neglecting the importance of memorising the Word, but he was indicating that only the Holy Spirit can reveal the living Word in you (John 1:1).

The Spirit can use a Scripture that we have read a hundred times before and open our eyes to see it in a way that we had never comprehended before. When the Holy Spirit anoints and inspires the Bible, He will lead us to become more like Christ.

"The supreme end of the Holy Spirit's indwelling and in-working is to manifest the person of Christ, as consciously possessed by us and possessing us," preached the Rev. Evan Hopkins. "This is the mystery, 'Christ in you.' The Holy Spirit takes of the things of Christ and shows them to the believer; He testifies to Christ; He glorifies Christ. He shows Christ in all His offices and relations; He makes Him real as our actual possession; He clothes Him with glorious attractions, so that, gazing on Him, we are enamoured of His Divine charms. It is one thing to have Christ revealed without, as a historic personage, and another thing to have Him revealed within, as our Master, Lord, Friend. The Word of God can and does hold Him up and sets Him forth before us, crucified for our sake; but only the Spirit of God can reveal Him within us, as manifest and indwelling."[3]

We can memorise parts of the Bible, but only the Holy Spirit can make us live like Jesus. It was often said of Rees Howells that he learnt the Bible as the Spirit made him live it! We need a similar experience. For example, the Bible states that we shall reap as we sow: 'Do not be deceived, God is not mocked; for whatever a man sows, that he will also reap' (Galatians 6:7). We may read this Scripture over and over again and never understand it; but the Holy Spirit can reveal to us the many aspects of its meaning. One disciple learnt that this Scripture can be applied to all areas of our lives. In forgiving (Matthew 6:4-15), in judging (Matthew 7:1-2), in giving (Luke 6:37-38), in tithing (Malachi 3:10), and in hearing and responding (Mark 4:24-25) etc.

"The Holy Spirit will reveal great truths to us from the Bible and with personal revelation which will always coincide with the teaching of Scripture," said a disciple of the Lord. "Once I was praying and telling the Lord how much I loved Him, when the Holy Spirit responded saying, 'You only love Me in measure.' I was shocked by what He said, and as I dwelt on this, I began to learn that my love and obedience to the Lord is measured. As a direct response to my faith, God's answer will be equal to my willingness to measure up to His Word in obedience. If my obedience is limited, God's response, if any, will match mine. However, if I respond with full obedience, God will respond in all His fullness.

"As the Spirit continued teaching me, I learnt that my life in Christ is in many ways, based upon the measure of my willingness to cooperate with the Spirit to allow Him to guide, teach and train me. If I obey the Word of the Lord and follow His direct leadings with a full measure of obedience, I shall reap the same. But if I give a small measure of obedience, I shall reap little.

"God in His eternal plan for the world will not waste time forever with believers who give Him partial obedience. God said, 'My Spirit shall not strive with man forever' (Genesis 6:3). At one point we must all choose – His way or ours; obedience or endless rebellion."

"The Holy Spirit in His role as Divine Teacher expects us to believe Him and step out in faith when He gives us personal guidance," said a disciple of the Lord. "The Holy Spirit spoke to me about ending a friendship with a Christian who was very negative, backbiting and critical of all (2 Thessalonians 3:6, 1 Timothy 6:4-5). I was hesitant to obey, but knew I had no choice and as God separated us, I realised how his negative spirit had been deeply effecting me. This man was not happy that I was not fellowshipping with him any more, but as I learnt, it was not real fellowship, but backbiting on his behalf. More than a decade later, I have served the Lord in the most wonderful ways, when I met this man again, and I found he was still in a bad rut. Through this I learnt that whenever the Spirit asks us to do something that does not make any sense, He expects us to step out in faith, with the knowledge that He knows something about the future which is impossible for us to know at that point.

"As God, He does not need to explain the reasons for all He asks us to do. When the Holy Spirit speaks to a Christian and says, 'I want you to end this friendship,' it is not because God does not want him or her to be happy, but because God sees the future (Proverbs 13:20). He knows the pain that will result in trying to keep alive a dead friendship, which will or has already become destructive to God's will and purposes."

The Holy Spirit will guide us into all truth and will reveal any lesson in God's Word that we need to learn and apply in our daily lives. When we are in a test, the Holy Spirit will guide us to focus our minds on God's promises in the Bible (John 14:26). But if we focus on the test and are not abiding in faith, emotional discouragement will begin to undermine our standard of faith in Christ. Therefore, when we focus on God's promises, His Word, His power, and His ability to intervene the test will seem smaller.

During the Welsh Revival (1904-1905), Evan Roberts explained that he was being led and guided by the Holy Spirit. "The movement is not of me, it is of God," said Evan. "I would not dare to try to direct it. Obey the Spirit, that is our word in everything. It is the Spirit alone which is leading us in our meetings and in all that is done."

*Questions to consider:* Have you invited the Holy Spirit to be your Teacher and Guide? Are your spiritual ears open to hear what the Holy Spirit wants to teach you?

*Actions:* Ask the Holy Spirit to lead and guide you. Ask Him to be your Teacher.

# Chapter Sixteen

## The Spirit Speaks, Guides and Sends Forth

- Jesus said, "For the Holy Spirit will teach you at that time what you should say" (Luke 12:12).
- 'The Spirit said to Philip, "Go near and overtake this chariot" ' (Acts 8:29).
- 'Now when they came up out of the water, the Spirit of the Lord caught Philip away, so that the eunuch saw him no more; and he went on his way rejoicing' (Acts 8:39).
- 'While Peter thought about the vision, the Spirit said to him, "Behold, three men are seeking you. Arise therefore, go down and go with them, doubting nothing; for I have sent them" ' (Acts 10:19-20).
- "Then the Spirit told me to go with them, doubting nothing. Moreover these six brethren accompanied me and we entered the man's house" (Acts 11:12).
- 'Then one of them, named Agabus, stood up and showed by the Spirit that there was going to be a great famine throughout all the world, which also happened in the days of Claudius Caesar' (Acts 11:28).
- 'As they ministered to the Lord and fasted, the Holy Spirit said, "Now separate to Me Barnabas and Saul for the work to which I have called them" ' (Acts 13:2).
- 'So, being sent out by the Holy Spirit, they went down to Seleucia, and from there they sailed to Cyprus' (Acts 13:4).
- 'For it seemed good to the Holy Spirit and to us, to lay upon you no greater burden than these necessary things' (Acts 15:28).
- 'They were forbidden by the Holy Spirit to preach the Word in Asia…they tried to go into Bithynia, but the Spirit did not permit them' (Acts 16:6-7).
- "The Holy Spirit testifies in every city, saying…" (Acts 20:23).
- 'They told Paul through the Spirit not to go up to Jerusalem' (Acts 21:4).
- 'When Agabus had come to us, he took Paul's belt, bound his own hands and feet, and said, "Thus says the Holy Spirit, 'So shall the Jews at Jerusalem bind the man who owns this belt and deliver him into the hands of the Gentiles' " ' (Acts 21:11-12).
- "The Holy Spirit spoke rightly through Isaiah the prophet to our fathers…" (Acts 28:25).

# Chapter Seventeen

## The Spotlight of Holiness

If we choose to walk with the Holy Spirit and desire to be enrolled in His school of living faith, His desire is to bring our lives up to His standards. He is holy, therefore He will lead us into holy living. To do this, the Holy Spirit will put His spotlight on our lives and lead us to forsake sin (Proverbs 28:13). James explained that the Holy Spirit, as Christ's representative on earth is like a holy jealous husband. We are Christ's bride and He does not want to share us with another: 'Adulterers and adulteresses! Do you not know that friendship with the world is enmity with God? Whoever therefore wants to be a friend of the world makes himself an enemy of God. Or do you think that the Scripture says in vain, "The Spirit who dwells in us yearns jealously?" ' (James 4:4-5).

The Holy Spirit showed Rees Howells that He expected him to live to a far higher standard than others, even decent religious people. If the Holy Spirit is to fill every area of our lives, we also will need to surrender every area to Him, for us to live the higher life, as Rees Howells did. To do this, the Holy Spirit will not only point out sin in our lives, but He will also tell us to give up seemly 'neutral' aspects of our lives, that have become idols or unknown stumbling blocks.

"When the Holy Spirit started dealing with me, He began to point out sins in my life," said a disciple of the Lord. "But as the years went on, He began to ask me to give up many of my hobbies and interests, so that I could spend that time on His work."

Many who have walked with the Lord discover that the Holy Spirit will ask us to lay down things that we like or love on His altar. When they are laid on the altar, the fire of the Lord descends and takes the sacrifice. This is the process of purging our old lives, to lay an essential foundation for the Lord to become our Rock. To drink the new wine of the Kingdom, we need new wineskins (Mark 2:22).

'There is a great difference between saying that we are prepared to live our lives according to the dictates of the Lord Jesus, and saying that the Lord can rule our lives for us,' wrote Dr. Kurt Koch. 'This is what He waits for – the command to take over. If we hope to stand in the battle, Jesus must become the Lord of our time, the Lord of our strength, the Lord of our wills, the Lord of our possessions, the Lord of our plans, and the Lord of our decisions. Jesus said in Matthew 11:27, "All things have been delivered to Me by My Father." '[1] We must ask ourselves, does this include us? Only when Jesus is our Lord will He protect us from the lordship of others

(Romans 8:31, 1 John 4:4).

The answer of religion to the carnal nature is to make a set of rules and regulations which all must follow. But the Bible reveals that we must welcome the Holy Spirit into our lives, and His love, joy and peace will become so precious to us that we will not want to live in sin (Philippians 3:8).

The true price of sin is alienation from God and when we have felt the Holy Spirit's peace, we will never want to lose it again. Walking with Him in the light brings far more pleasure than sin once did. Paul describes this process: 'Walk in the Spirit and you shall not fulfil the lust of the flesh. For the flesh lusts against the Spirit and the Spirit against the flesh; and these are contrary to one another, so that you do not do the things that you wish. But if you are led by the Spirit, you are not under the law. Now the works of the flesh are evident, which are: adultery, fornication, uncleanness, lewdness, idolatry, sorcery, hatred, contentions, jealousies, outbursts of wrath, selfish ambitions, dissensions, heresies, envy, murders, drunkenness, revelries and the like; of which I tell you beforehand, just as I also told you in time past, that those who practice such things will not inherit the Kingdom of God. But the fruit of the Spirit is love, joy, peace, longsuffering, kindness, goodness, faithfulness, gentleness, self-control. Against such there is no law. And those who are Christ's have crucified the flesh with its passions and desires. If we live in the Spirit, let us also walk in the Spirit' (Galatians 5:16-25).

We are reminded once again of the revelation the Holy Spirit gave to one man who was praying and declaring his love for God when the Holy Spirit said, "You only love me in measure." This man was concerned, even offended by what the Spirit of God said to him. Nonetheless, he had learnt that when the Lord shows us something, it is foolish to argue with Him. When the Holy Spirit asks a question, it's not because He does not know the answer! He wants to reveal something to us. In these cases, we must let the revelation slip past the filter of our minds and into our spirit. Then when we have received the truth we can respond.

When this disciple pondered more about what the Holy Spirit said, it was revealed that the measure of our love for the Lord God will determine our willingness to be obedient to His will. Jesus taught that if we love Him, we will obey Him (John 15:1-17, Revelation 3:18-20). This teaches us that the more we love Him, the more willing we are to obey Him. When we obey Him, our love for Christ will be proven, and we will begin to learn how to abide and remain in the Vine of God (John 15).

The Bible gives us many warnings concerning our relationship with the Holy Spirit. We must not grieve the Holy Spirit (Ephesians 4:30-31), resist the Holy Spirit (Proverbs 29:1, Acts 7:51), nor quench the Holy Spirit (1 Thessalonians 5:19-20). Many people struggle to know what the will of God for their lives is, but the Scripture is very clear. 'For this is the will of God, your sanctification' (1 Thessalonians 4:3), and, 'Be conformed to the image of His Son' (Romans 8:20). God wants us to live like Him and a great part of that transformation takes place in the mind: 'In everything give thanks, for this is the will of God in Christ' (1 Thessalonians 5:18).

"After walking with the Lord for some time, the Holy Spirit showed me I had to get rid of all my secular music," said a disciple of the Lord. "These albums dated back to the 1960s and were worth a lot, just like the books of the early Christians (Acts 19:19). I threw them away and started worshipping instead. Then, as time drew on, I found when I was walking, driving and working, my spirit was singing songs to the Lord Jesus and I was more sensitive to the Holy Spirit's voice (Ephesians 5:19-20).

"I came to understand that all the 'noise' of the world had clouded out my sensitivity to the Holy Spirit; many of these artists had given themselves over to spirits of lust, rebellion, rage and hatred of God, and their lyrics were once repeated in my mind. Now I was singing songs in the Spirit to the Lord, instead of supporting ungodly artists whose music promotes antichrist lifestyles."

If we choose to live in the mud and mire of sin, we can't expect the Dove to fly with us (Luke 3:22). The Dove will fly away and leave us in the mess we have created. The Holy Spirit will only abide with those who desire holiness. In the Old Testament, the Holy Spirit came upon many people, but their sins led to Him leaving them (Judges 16:20, Romans 15:4). They had not learnt to abide with the Lord. But when Jesus came, the sign that He was the Messiah was that the Holy Spirit would remain upon Him. The Holy Spirit would not come upon Him and leave, but remain: 'Upon whom you see the Spirit descending and remaining...' (John 1:33).

"The Spirit of God has a will and desires," said a disciple of the Lord. "It took me some time to understand that we can set our minds and desires on the will of our flesh, or on the will of the Spirit. This is exactly what Paul taught the Romans. 'Those who live according to the flesh have their minds set on what the flesh desires; but those who live in accordance with the Spirit have their minds set on what the Spirit desires' " (Romans 8:5).

Does the Spirit of God remain in our lives? Do we abide in Him? Remember, the sign that Peter and John were called by God was not human qualifications on paper, but an acknowledgement that they had been with Jesus: 'Now when they saw the boldness of Peter and John, and perceived that they were uneducated and untrained men, they marvelled. And they realised that they had been with Jesus' (Acts 4:13).

In the New Testament there are constant warnings to resist sin and live holy lives. People sin because they enjoy the passing pleasure of sin (Hebrews 11:25), yet Paul knew the joy of the Spirit is more satisfying than anything else: 'Do not be drunk with wine, in which is dissipation; but be filled with the Spirit' (Ephesians 5:18). In Greek 'be filled' means to 'keep on being filled constantly and continually.' This indicates we can always make more room for God to fill us and the more we give to God of our lives, the more He can fill. Paul desired that the Ephesians would give all of themselves to God and be possessed by the Holy Spirit, because he prayed that they 'may be filled with all the fullness of God' (Ephesians 3:19).

"All Christians have received a deposit of the Holy Spirit within the vault of their hearts," said a disciple of the Lord. "That vault has been filled so far with sin, rebellion, pride and all manifestations of self. The Holy Spirit, as the new owner wants to clear that vault of all that is worldly, sinful and of self, and fill it with Himself."

'Holiness of heart and life means a definite separation from sin and worldly ways of living,' wrote J.A. Broadbelt, the Principal of Cliff College in the 1930s. 'Fellowship with Jesus means there are places to which we cannot go, books we cannot read, things we cannot do, and company we cannot keep...This detachment and separation from sin is necessary for our spiritual safety, and our effective work and witness to the Christian way of living...climbing with Jesus will mean for you and me a break and detachment from the sin of the world, and from many of the silly and frivolous things that are allowed in connection with some of our churches. This is the price we shall have to pay for spiritual power, spiritual revival and blessing.'[2]

"As a Christian for many years I wanted to live a holy life," said a disciple of the Lord. "I tried so hard in the flesh to think good thoughts, to stand in faith and to be righteous; yet the desires of the world seemed far more interesting and stronger than my will to be holy. The bright lights of the city made the Bible seem dull and the world tried to convince me I was missing out on much pleasure by trying to live holy. However, after I opened my life to the power of the Holy Spirit to have supremacy in my life, I felt His peace, joy and love – then the world lost much of its attraction. I did not want to sin, because I did not want to lose God's peace, joy and love in the Holy Spirit. The world once appeared as a delicious apple pie and every time I ate of it, it tasted good, but I ended up feeling sick. Now I have become tired of feeling sick and I am addicted to His peace."

When deciding if something is sin or not, the Rev. Evan Hopkins, gave his opinion that we must look to the Holy Spirit to lead us. "I have no doubt that God's Holy Spirit is now speaking to you," he preached, "and you say, 'I suppose that thing is a weight.' Yes, you know all about it; it is a weight; it does interfere with your progress and your growth. 'Other people do it.' Yes, but is it a weight, a hindrance to you? Lay it aside. 'Well, I have been praying about it. I believe in progressive sanctification and I am going to do it gradually.' Ah, that won't do; this is not a gradual, but the instantaneous side of sanctification. If you lay aside a weight, it drops. There is let-go faith as well as lay-hold faith. I do not need to put my finger upon it; I want the Holy Spirit to do that. It may be that, at the end, some of you will be coming to ask whether there is any harm in this or that. I am not going to answer you. Settle it with God and give Him the benefit of the doubt. Put away from you, therefore, every evil thing. You want the fullness of the Spirit. Well, now, this is God's way. We have to clear the way."

"Many churches have tried to make up rules for holiness," said a disciple of the Lord. "These rules have become a straightjacket of suppression for young Christians, who failing to live up to the standard of not doing 'this, that or the other' (Mark 7:7), find it easier to backslide. Paul wrote that all our rules 'have an appearance of wisdom,' and called this 'self-imposed religion,' but it has no power (Colossians 2:20-23).

"The gospel is not 'do not touch, taste or handle,' but repent and meet Jesus! Remember, 'the letter kills, but the Spirit gives life' (2 Corinthians 3:6). If we stopped handing out rule books, and encouraged all to meet with Jesus and welcome the Holy Spirit into their lives, His fire will change them and the world will be seen for what it truly is – empty and lost. When people see Christ in His power, they will begin to become indifferent to the world, because Christ's light is brighter than any lights in the city. It is oppression that we get from the world and liberty in Jesus Christ.

"We have not been called to meet a standard of holiness to see the Lord, we have been called to meet the Lord in repentance and faith, and then when we have seen Him, we shall want to live holy. When the holy fire of God descends on our lives, we shall desire holiness because the world, the flesh and the devil can never replicate an encounter with God. The gospel is good news, why then do we paint it as bad news by our self-imposed religion?"

*Questions to consider:* Has the Holy Spirit been speaking to you about something which is wrong in your life? Will you resist the Holy Spirit or obey Him?

*Actions:* Make a decision today to obey the Holy Spirit and allow Him to shine His spotlight of holiness in your life.

# Chapter Eighteen

## The Holy Spirit Preparing for Christ

### Jesus Conceived by the Holy Spirit
- "The Holy Spirit will come upon you and the power of the Highest will overshadow you; therefore, that Holy One who is to be born will be called the Son of God" (Luke 1:35).
- 'Now the birth of Jesus Christ was as follows: After His mother Mary was betrothed to Joseph, before they came together, she was found with child of the Holy Spirit' (Matthew 1:18).
- 'But while he thought about these things, behold, an angel of the Lord appeared to him in a dream, saying, "Joseph, son of David, do not be afraid to take to you Mary your wife, for that which is conceived in her is of the Holy Spirit" ' (Matthew 1:20).

### The Holy Spirit Preparing the Way For Christ
- John the Baptist "will be great in the sight of the Lord…he will also be filled with the Holy Spirit, even from his mother's womb" (Luke 1:15).
- 'It happened when Elizabeth heard the greeting of Mary, that the babe leaped in her womb and Elizabeth was filled with the Holy Spirit' (Luke 1:41).
- 'Now his father Zacharias was filled with the Holy Spirit' (Luke 1:67).
- 'There was a man in Jerusalem whose name was Simeon, and this man was just and devout…and the Holy Spirit was upon him. And it had been revealed to him by the Holy Spirit that he would not see death before he had seen the Lord's Christ. So he came by the Spirit into the temple' (Luke 2:25-27).

### The Witness of the Holy Spirit
- John the Baptist said, "I indeed baptise you with water unto repentance, but He who is coming after me is mightier than I, whose sandals I am not worthy to carry. He will baptise you with the Holy Spirit and fire" (Matthew 3:11).
- 'When He had been baptised, Jesus came up immediately from the water; and behold, the heavens were opened to Him, and He saw the Spirit of God descending like a dove and alighting upon Him' (Matthew 3:16).

# Chapter Nineteen

## Gifts of the Holy Spirit

When the Holy Spirit comes upon us, we need to welcome Him in all His fullness and we will receive the revelation from God, that He is not only our Teacher and Guide, but also the Gift Giver. Paul wrote about the gifts of the Spirit: 'For to one is given the word of wisdom through the Spirit, to another the word of knowledge through the same Spirit, to another faith by the same Spirit, to another the gifts of healing by the same Spirit, to another the working of miracles, to another prophecy, to another discerning of spirits, to another different kinds of tongues, to another the interpretation of tongues' (1 Corinthians 12:8-10).

The gifts of the Spirit are very important to the Church, because it was supernaturally brought to birth by the outpouring of the Holy Spirit and it must be supernaturally edified and grown (1 Corinthians 14:3). It was the Spirit who drew sinners to Jesus, who convicted them and He led them to saving faith in Christ. Therefore, the Spirit of God is needed in the Church to exercise His gifts to disciple and encourage them also (1 Corinthians 14:12).

There are nine gifts of the Spirit and the following describes some of their functions.

1. Wisdom: Supernatural ability to apply knowledge, experience or insight in specific situations. The believer grasps Divine insight from God (Genesis 40:12, 41:25-38, 2 Kings 4:38-41, 20:7, Acts 8:9-23, 13:6-12).

2. Knowledge: The ability to receive specific information given as a direct revelation from God (2 Kings 1:17, 6:8-12, 20:1-11, Mark 2:8, Acts 10:19, 11:12).

3. Faith: The ability to believe for something, which is naturally impossible. This extraordinary confidence in God is not shaken by situations, pain, apparent failure, or ridicule (1 Kings 18:21-40, Acts 12:5-16). Faith is a gift of the Spirit and it is also a fruit of the Spirit!

4. Healing: Gifts of healing is plural (1 Corinthians 12:9). These gifts are given to release Divine restoration of people to health. As there are more than one gift of healing, some people's gift or anointing may be greater in one area – for example healing of backs or legs (2 Kings 5:1-17, Acts 3:1-11).

5. Miracles: The ability to do supernatural works of power to glorify Jesus Christ the Lord (Acts 19:11-12, Galatians 3:5, Hebrews 2:4).

6. Prophecy: This is the ability to receive direct revelation from God and then to communicate that revelation to others (1 Kings

17:1, Acts 11:28). A prophet 'hears' a word in his or her spirit and releases the word from God to others. The prophet will have to spend a lot of time waiting on God, in His presence.

7. Discernment of spirits: The supernatural ability to discern what is true and what is false; this includes discerning the difference between God's Spirit and individual evil spirits (1 Kings 22:19-23, Matthew 10:1, Mark 5:1-20, Luke 9:37-42, Acts 16:16-18).

8. Tongues: The ability to speak in a spiritual heavenly language (Acts 2:4, 10:46, 19:6). We can pray in tongues for private prayer and edification, and the gift can be manifested in meetings with interpretation following. When we pray in tongues the Holy Spirit can bypass the mind ~~and pray perfect prayers~~. Tongues release us from the limits of human language (1 Corinthians 14:4).

9. Interpretation of Tongues: The ability to interpret tongues into a 'known' language (1 Corinthians 14:2, 22-28, 39). We speak the mysteries of God as we interpret the tongue into a known language.

The gifts of the Spirit are given by God to help build up and edify the body of Christ, to equip the Church for ministry. Usually the gifts are manifested when Christians meet together, but not exclusively. Someone could give a prophecy, or a tongue and an interpretation should follow, as took place in the early church (1 Corinthians 12:4-12, 14:26, 32-33, 39-40, Ephesians 4:12, 1 Peter 4:10).

"The Holy Spirit gives His gifts to the people He chooses," said a disciple of the Lord. "He can give a word of wisdom and knowledge to anyone. I believe He has given me these when I needed specific wisdom for a breakthrough to serve Him. I also believe He gave me Divine words of knowledge, beyond any 'human evidence,' when praying for people.

"The gifts of faith, healing and miracles are usually exercised by people who have asked for these seeking the Lord; not all tend to have these. Have you ever met someone who has such powerful faith and can believe in anything impossible coming to pass for God's glory? That person has the gift of faith, and usually healing and miracles will follow. However, faith is also a fruit of the Spirit which must be developed by all and allowed to flow. With the gifts of healing and miracles, often God raises up specific people or ministries ~~that focus on them.~~ We can all pray for healing and miracles, but some have more grace than others.

"The gift of prophecy can come to all; however it usually resides on someone who is called to be a prophet. In the New Testament Church there were several who were prophets (Acts 15:32, 21:9-11, Ephesians 4:11). In its simplest form prophesying is hearing from God and speaking it out. For this reason Paul encouraged the members of the early church to seek to prophesy (1 Corinthians 14:1, 24-26, 31, 39). However, as there are many deceiving spirits in operation, we need the gift of discernment to learn what comes from God and what is from a demonic origin (2 Corinthians 11:14, 1 Timothy 4:1). We must test all things (1 Thessalonians 5:21).

"The gift of private tongues is the most exercised gift and I believe all can have it, if they cry out to God and open their mouths asking God to fill them! Then, the gift of interpretation of tongues in a meeting, usually comes when someone steps out in faith and speaks out in tongues, as the Spirit moves, and another interprets what God says. The first time I gave an interpretation of a tongue, I had two or three words placed into my spirit by God. I knew if I spoke them out the rest would come. It took faith for me to step out and speak in front of all, and as I did, the words of God flowed."

Christians often feel too small for God to use them, but the gifts of the Spirit can be given to every Christian who seeks for them and is willing to receive. Hudson Taylor, founder of the China Inland Mission knew God seeks out 'insignificant' people to use. "God was looking for someone small enough to use and found me," he said. This can often be the testimony of those who exercise the gifts.

"I wanted to speak in tongues because I knew the Holy Spirit wants to give this gift to His children," said a disciple of the Lord. "I started praising God in English and suddenly, I began to speak in an unknown language. It felt a little bit strange at first and I knew I could stop it, but instead, I let the Holy Spirit expand my vocabulary – it was the Spirit of God praying in and through me."

Tongues are the most common of the gifts, but all of the gifts can be manifested today, and when we invite the Spirit of God into our lives, we also invite Him to exercise His right to use His gifts!

"During a time of prayer and worship, I had the first few words of a prophecy hanging on the tip of my tongue," said a disciple of the Lord. "I knew if I spoke them out the Spirit would give me more; but I had to take a leap of faith and speak them out loud in front of others. It's the same with exercising the gift of tongues in a meeting. The Holy Spirit stirs me up inside and I have to 'get out of the boat,' like Peter. Then when I open my mouth to speak out what He gives, He gives me more. After the tongue ceases, I then wait for the Holy Spirit to move someone else to interpret the tongue."

Paul warned that we should not be ignorant about spiritual gifts (1 Corinthians 12:1). We must remember that these gifts are given by God and they are a demonstration of the power of the Holy Spirit working amongst us. They are His gifts and He manifests them for the glory of God! If we belittle them, we belittle the work of God.

"The gifts of the Holy Spirit are given to people who ask for them," said a disciple of the Lord Jesus. "The Holy Spirit will choose what gifts He wants to give to people, however I do believe all can speak in tongues if they want to. The reason for this is because the gift of private tongues for edification is one of the gifts we can all exercise without the direct leading of God (1 Corinthians 14:4). I cannot get a word of knowledge or wisdom unless the Holy Spirit gives it to me; yet I can pray in tongues for edification at any time. The first time I spoke in tongues was when I asked believers to lay hands on me and pray for the gift to be given. I opened my mouth praising God in English and then strange sounds followed. I felt nervous and maybe a little embarrassed, that it may not be real, but as I progressed, more came and over the following weeks the language developed as the Holy Spirit enabled. When you speak your first few words in a new language you do not become fluent immediately; it was the same for me with tongues. Everyday I had to practise and still today I pray everyday, and it is the Spirit praying!"

Paul explained these gifts and other are distributed by the Holy Spirit as He wills among believers: 'Having gifts differing according to the grace given to us, let us use them: if prophecy, let us prophesy in proportion to our faith; or ministry, let us use it in our ministering; he who teaches, in teaching; he who exhorts, in exhortation; he who gives, with liberality; he who leads, with diligence; he who shows mercy, with cheerfulness...distributing to the needs of the saints, given to hospitality' (Romans 12:6-8, 13).

Paul also explains the structure of the Church: 'God has appointed these in the Church: first apostles, second prophets, third teachers, after that miracles, then gifts of healings, helps, administrations, varieties of tongues' (1 Corinthians 12:28). 'But to each one grace was given according to the measure of Christ's gift. And He Himself gave some to be apostles, some prophets, some evangelists, and some pastors and teachers. For the equipping of the saints for the work of the ministry' (Ephesians 4:7, 11-12).

"Once someone told me never to tell them about God ever again," said a disciple of the Lord. "He was very angry because he had lost two babies in miscarriages and his wife was about to lose a third. Then suddenly out of my mouth came, 'It's very simple my friend. If you will only go outside, get down on your knees and cry out to God, the baby will live!' I was amazed at what I said and the non-believer followed these instructions, and the baby was saved and so was he. As I thought about this later, I understood it was not me speaking; it was the Holy Spirit speaking through me. Jesus told us the Spirit would speak through us when we were put in pressured situations for His sake (Mark 13:11-12). I was His channel and when the man cried out to God, the Holy Spirit moved and Christ saved the child, and the man was 'saved' too!"

Jesus often moved in the gifts of the Spirit when He ministered (Isaiah 11:1-2). He often used words of knowledge (John 1:48, 4:17-18), gifts of healing and miracles (Matthew 4:23, Luke 6:19, Acts 10:38), wisdom (Matthew 11:19, 13:54, Mark 6:2), discernment of spirits (Matthew 8:16), and prophecy (Matthew 25:1-46), etc.

The apostles operated in the gifts of the Spirit and their testimony is recorded in Scripture. Paul shared how non-believers can be convicted by the Holy Spirit when a prophecy is given: 'But if all prophesy and an unbeliever or an uninformed person comes in, he is convinced by all, he is convicted by all' (1 Corinthians 14:24).

James also explains how the gifts of healing can operate: 'Is anyone among you sick? Let him call for the elders of the church, and let them pray over him, anointing him with oil in the name of the Lord. And the prayer of faith will save the sick, and the Lord will raise him up. And if he has committed sins, he will be forgiven. Confess your trespasses to one another and pray for one another, that you may be healed. The effective, fervent prayer of a righteous man avails much' (James 5:14-16).

The gifts of the Holy Spirit are only to be used for the glory of God and sometimes they come for a season. It is unusual for a Christian to have all the gifts exercising in his or her life, as most believers only have a few. However, we are warned that these gifts can cease if we misuse them or allow ourselves to walk away from God into sin, or if Christians and churches despise them (Isaiah 52:11, Matthew 12:18, Luke 3:22, Romans 1:11, 11:29, 12:6, 1 Corinthians 12-14, Hebrews 2:4, Peter 1:16, 2 Timothy 1:6).

The gifts of the Spirit are given by God for the edification of all, but one of the great problems of the Charismatic and Pentecostal churches has often been people exercising the gifts, whilst not living holy lives. God in His grace has often blessed, but like the church at Corinth we have often devalued these wonderful gifts from God by our worldly lifestyles (1 Corinthians 3:3, James 4:4).

Christians can often be like King Saul in the Old Testament; the Holy Spirit came upon him several times and he prophesied, yet because he refused to let the Spirit deal with his sin and self, he ended up far from God and fell into deception (1 Samuel 10:11-12, 19:24, 28:6-7). It is important to understand that moving in the gifts of the Spirit is not a sign of spiritual maturity, but of God's grace. The gifts of the Spirit do not represent the favour of God on our lives and lifestyles – do not be deceived! 'For the gifts and the calling of God are irrevocable' (Romans 11:29).

Sadly, in many churches, the Holy Spirit as a Person and Gift Giver is not welcomed. Dr. Carl Henry wrote: 'In twentieth century Christianity the Holy Spirit is still a displaced Person... whenever the Church makes the Spirit of God a refugee, the Church, not the Spirit becomes the vagabond.'

God the Father sent His Son into the world to reconcile it to Him, and the Son sent the Spirit to continue His ministry (John 3:16, 15:26). Therefore, if the Holy Spirit is not welcome in a church He will withdraw into silence and the congregation will be left with rituals, powerless preaching and empty ceremonies, until it closes (Galatians 3:2-4, Colossians 2:16-17, 21-23, Revelation 1:20, 2:5).

When Peter preached at Cornelius' home, he explained how the Trinity worked in unity to demonstrate the power of God and fulfil God's will: 'God (the Father) anointed Jesus of Nazareth (the Son) with the Holy Spirit and with power, who went about doing good and healing all who were oppressed by the devil' (Acts 10:38).

"The Father sent the Son, therefore no one can come to or receive the Father apart from the Son," taught Derek Prince (1 John 2:23, 5:12). "But also, the Son sent the Holy Spirit, therefore no-one can come to receive from the Son except through the Spirit."[1]

The gifts of the Spirit are supernatural. Sometimes Christians are afraid of this word, but in the Christian context, supernatural means that which is above natural human ability. When God changes anyone's life – it is a supernatural act, beyond the natural!

Some churches have become afraid of the gifts of the Spirit, but we must be reminded that God has not given us a spirit of fear (Romans 8:15, 2 Timothy 1:7). The fear of the gifts of the Spirit is a tool Satan uses to keep Christians devoid of the Spirit's power. Satan is afraid when we exercise God's gifts as the Lord wants! The gifts are given because there is a job to be done, and only the Holy Spirit can do this job, and He chooses to work through us!

One reason why God has given the gifts of the Spirit is because non-believers are hungry for supernatural demonstrations of the power of God. When they come into a church meeting and find empty ceremony, they may never return and go to the devil's agents instead, seeking his supernatural power. The Bible forbids us from using or seeking witches, warlocks, druids, tarot cards, spiritualists, sorcerers, mediums, horoscopes, spells, incantations, etc., (Deuteronomy 18:10-14); yet even Christians have sought these when local churches refuse to allow God to exercise His right as the Gift Giver! God hates all these because seeking insight or aid from any source other than God is idolatry and all other supernatural power is Satanic in origin (John 10:10, Acts 13:9, Revelation 16:14).

*Questions to consider:* Do you move in the gifts of the Spirit? Do you need to seek the Holy Spirit to give you His gifts? Do you need to step out in faith and exercise the gifts God has given to you?

*Actions:* Set aside some time to ask God to give you the gifts of the Spirit and opportunities to use them for Christ's glory.

# Chapter Twenty

## The Holy Spirit in the Life of Christ

### Leading, Testing and Empowering
- 'Then Jesus was led up by the Spirit into the wilderness to be tempted by the devil' (Matthew 4:1).
- 'Then Jesus returned in the power of the Spirit to Galilee, and news of Him went out through all the surrounding region' (Luke 4:14).
- Jesus said, "The Spirit of the Lord is upon Me, because He has anointed Me to preach the gospel to the poor. He has sent Me to heal the broken-hearted, to proclaim liberty to the captives and recovery of sight to the blind, to set at liberty those who are oppressed" (Luke 4:18).

### Confronting the Enemy and Warnings
- Jesus said, "But if I cast out demons by the Spirit of God, surely the Kingdom of God has come upon you" (Matthew 12:28).
- Jesus said, "Therefore I say to you, every sin and blasphemy will be forgiven men, but the blasphemy against the Spirit will not be forgiven men. Anyone who speaks a word against the Son of Man, it will be forgiven him; but whoever speaks against the Holy Spirit, it will not be forgiven him, either in this age or in the age to come" (Matthew 12:31-32).

### The Spirit Given Without Measure in Christ's Life
- 'A shoot will come up from the stump of Jesse; from his roots a Branch will bear fruit. The Spirit of the Lord will rest on Him, the Spirit of wisdom and of understanding, the Spirit of counsel and of might, the Spirit of the knowledge and fear of the Lord' (Isaiah 11:1-2).
- Jesus said, "For He whom God has sent speaks the Words of God, for God does not give the Spirit by measure" (John 3:34).
- Peter said, "God anointed Jesus of Nazareth with the Holy Spirit and with power, who went about doing good and healing all who were oppressed by the devil, for God was with Him" (Acts 10:38).

### The Holy Spirit in Redemption
- 'How much more shall the blood of Christ, who through the eternal Spirit offered Himself without spot to God...' (Hebrews 9:14).

## Chapter Twenty-One

## The Fruit of the Holy Spirit

Samuel Rees Howells lived through the days of the Charismatic renewal and knew some of the British pioneers of Pentecostal Christianity. Nevertheless, he was concerned that many believers were making the exact same mistakes as the Corinthians. He was perplexed that many had become infatuated with the gifts of the Spirit, but they had never truly met the Person of the Spirit. Had any of these believers been taught that there is a great battle going on between their wills and the will of the Holy Spirit? 'For the flesh lusts against the Spirit and the Spirit against the flesh; and these are contrary to one another' (Galatians 5:17). God's Spirit, we are told, will not strive with us endlessly (Genesis 6:3), and we must choose to serve God with all our hearts (Psalm 103:9, 2 Corinthians 11:2).

There are nine gifts of the Spirit and there are nine manifestations of the fruit of the Holy Spirit to bring balance to the power, and produce the right character to exercise these gifts. The fruit of the Spirit is the character of Christ. Jesus said, "Therefore by their fruits you will know them" (Matthew 7:20), and we learn that, 'The fruit of the Spirit is love, joy, peace, longsuffering, kindness, goodness, faithfulness, gentleness and self-control' (Galatians 5:22-23). It's interesting to note there are many gifts, but there is only one fruit. Therefore, we cannot choose to have peace and ignore self-control. All the fruit wants to grow together as one, and we cannot have one without the other seeking to develop at the same time.

"The fruit of the Holy Spirit can only be manifested in our lives to the measure with which we are prepared to die and surrender to the Lord," said a disciple of the Lord. "I once had a wonderful baptism in the Holy Spirit and He overpowered my flesh life, but instead of agreeing with the change He was making in me, I allowed myself to go back to my old ways of living – and the change did not remain permanent. I learnt that we must bring our lives into agreement with what the Holy Spirit wants to do in us. If He comes in peace, we must walk in peace. If He comes in love, we must walk in love and so forth. This is what abiding in Christ means, to walk as He would walk (1 John 2:6). Our lives must come into agreement with His and we must follow in obedience. The result is this: 'You shall hide them in the secret place of Your presence' " (Psalm 31:20).

Before we became believers in Jesus Christ, our entire lives were dominated by how we felt, what we thought and what we wanted. We could go to bed feeling good and wake up feeling miserable, and that cloud could follow us all day and affect all the people who we came into contact with. In many ways, our lives were dominated by – "I feel, I want and I need." We were slaves to these inward desires of the flesh. Yet, when we became believers in Jesus, the seed of all that God is, was planted within our spirits (Ephesians 1:3). Deep inside of us, in our spirits, we became 'new creatures in Christ' (2 Corinthians 5:17, Galatians 6:15). However, the old creature, or self, or flesh (Ephesians 4:22), still dominated us as our souls (our minds, wills and emotions), still wanted to block out and vote on the will of God. We need to allow the Holy Spirit to renew our minds, so that our minds, wills and emotions will agree with the seed of God that was planted within us (Galatians 5:24).

We were once dominated by – "I feel, I want, I need," – but now the fruit of the Holy Spirit has been planted within us as a new seed and we must water that seed for it to grow. The fruit of the Spirit includes self-control and we must exercise this fruit by declaring, "I will not be controlled by my emotions anymore! How I feel does not need to affect my faith! No longer will my emotions manage me, I will manage them by the fruit of the Spirit." This declaration of faith can be the beginning of a long, up-hill walk to allow the fruit of the Holy Spirit to replace the fruit of the flesh in our lives!

"I never understood how I could be a new creature in Christ and still sin at the same time," said a disciple of the Lord. "Then I realised by reading Scripture, that it was my spirit that was born again (John 3:5-8). All the promises of God about me are all true and have been planted as a seed in my spirit. But my mind has to be renewed to think and act like my born again spirit wants it to. It's all in the Bible: 'The Spirit Himself bears witness with our spirit that we are children of God' (Romans 8:16). You see, the Spirit of God communicates with my born again spirit and now I must renew my mind to think like the Spirit wants me to (Romans 12:2). When the Bible says, 'If you live according to the flesh you will die' (Romans 8:13), it means the spiritual part of us will begin to die when we deliberately choose to reject God's will. This is why so many Christians never become disciples of Jesus and end up sounding exactly like the world. They have never allowed God's Spirit to overrule their flesh to exercise Christ's Lordship."

The Holy Spirit wishes to plant a new heart into our lives, a heart that seeks after His fruit: 'But the Holy Spirit also witnesses to us; for after He had said before, "...I will put My laws into their hearts, and in their minds I will write them" ' (Hebrews 10:15-16).

When the Holy Spirit comes into our lives, He will convict us of sin and will make us feel uncomfortable. He will bring to light our sinful ways, highlighting our need for the Saviour. This is the beginning of the process of the Holy Spirit revitalising our conscience, which has been seared by the hot iron, in sin (1 Timothy 4:2). For the first time, we begin to see sin for all that it is, and we like Isaiah cry out, "Woe is me, for I am undone. Because I am a man of unclean lips and I dwell in the midst of a people of unclean lips; for my eyes have seen the King, the Lord of Hosts" (Isaiah 6:5). After we have found the Saviour and believed on Him, the Holy Spirit will continue the work of revitalising our consciences, as we meditate on the Bible. Each day, as we set aside some time to read the Bible and be in prayer, we should see the standard God wants for us, and seek Him that His fruit will be manifest in our lives.

German opponent of Nazism and WWII martyr Dietrich Bonhoeffer (1906-1945), wrote: 'When Christ calls a man – He bids him come and die.' When we die to self, then the fruit of the Holy Spirit can replace what self once possessed. We are commanded by God to bear fruit within our lives (Matthew 3:8), because people will know us by our fruits – a changed character and lifestyle (Matthew 7:16). As we surrender every area to the Holy Spirit, our old negative ways will die (1 Corinthians 15:31), and as the carnal life is crucified, we will produce new fruit; the fruit of the Spirit (John 12:24).

"I once wondered how so many people blessed by the Holy Spirit could return to worldly living," said a disciple of the Lord. "Then I realised our lives are like jugs divided into sections and filled with dirty water. If we want these jugs to be filled with something pure – the fullness of the Holy Spirit – we will need to empty all the sections of their impurities of the world, sin and self, to make room for the new. The more room we make in our lives, the greater we can be filled with Him, because He cannot fill where self and sin is king."

"The water that Jesus gives shall become in him a well," said the Rev. Evan Hopkins (John 4:14). "Here we have a fresh experience of an old gift. You have had the water, but now it has become to you a spring overflowing, and the friction and strain have been taken out of your life. You say, 'Must I not make a desperate effort? No, let the Lord possess you, and the impatient man becomes gentle; He has Divine provision to meet the Divine requirement. But we cannot enter into these blessings unless in right relationship to God. Have we handed ourselves over to Him to be at His disposal? Many people have a faith that seeks, but not a faith that rests. The Lord is here, rest on Him."[1]

Duncan Campbell said in the Hebridean Revival (1949-1952), "An isolated act of surrender will guarantee nothing unless that act is initial to an attitude of surrender, continuous obedience and faith."[2]

As we surrender our old self or flesh to God and continually receive the infilling of His Spirit, the fruit of the Spirit should become a reality in our lives. This is not theory, but a daily experience in our everyday lives. All His fruit is manifested through love, as fruit is singular, not plural: 'The fruit of the Spirit is love, joy, peace, longsuffering, kindness, goodness, faithfulness, gentleness and self-control' (Galatians 5:22-23).

"Only God can take out of your heart the bad temper, pride, malice, revenge, love of the world, and all other evil things that have taken possession of it; and fill it with holy love and peace," said General William Booth (1829-1912), the founder of the Salvation Army. "To God you must look, to God you must go. This is the work of the Holy Spirit: He is the Purifying Fire; He is the Cleansing Flame."

To the greater extent that we allow the Holy Spirit to come into our lives and possess the areas our flesh once possessed, to that extent the fruit of the Spirit can be manifested through us.

"The Kingdom of God is not going to advance by our churches becoming filled with men," said one preacher, "but by men in our churches becoming filled with God." In the 1920s, Gideon L. Powell wrote something similar: "What is imperatively needed in evangelical churches today is a consuming passion to be filled with the fullness of God. The communion of the Holy Spirit means two things: His communion with us and our communion with Him. We must do as He would have us to do. Our thoughts, purposes and actions must be such that He can endorse. We must do what He suggests and commands, and no objection must be raised or resistance offered. There must be no grieving or quenching the Spirit...we must allow Him to express Himself in us and through us...Jesus was born of the Spirit, baptised of the Spirit, led of the Spirit into the wilderness, and returned in the power of the Spirit. Jesus declared that He did not speak of Himself but taught as prompted by the Spirit. Indeed, coming to the great act of His life, its very climax, as it were, we read that it was through the Eternal Spirit that Christ offered Himself on Calvary."[3]

"The Holy Spirit is the Person who puts reins on our flesh," said a disciple of the Lord. "It is He who convicts us from within and urges us to live like Christ. It is He who speaks to us in the secret place, when no-one else is around, and reminds us that our bodies are the temple of the Holy Spirit, and He is ever watching (1 Corinthians 6:13, 19). Only the Holy Spirit can aid us to crucify the flesh and allow His fruit to be manifested in its place."

*Questions to consider:* What areas of your life show the least fruit? How can you change?

*Actions:* Invite the Holy Spirit to replace your self nature with His fruit. Make a conscious decision to allow the fruit of the Spirit to manifest in your life, in your daily circumstances.

# Chapter Twenty-Two

# Hope in Christ Jesus

## We All Need the Holy Spirit
- 'While Peter was still speaking these words, the Holy Spirit fell upon all those who heard the Word...the gift of the Holy Spirit had been poured out on the Gentiles also. For they heard them speak with tongues and magnify God. Then Peter answered, "Can anyone forbid water, that these should not be baptised who have received the Holy Spirit just as we have?" ' (Acts 10:44-47).
- 'As I began to speak, the Holy Spirit fell upon them, as upon us at the beginning. Then I remembered the Word of the Lord, how He said, "John indeed baptised with water, but you shall be baptised with the Holy Spirit." If therefore God gave them the same gift as He gave us when we believed on the Lord Jesus Christ, who was I that I could withstand God?' (Acts 11:15-17).
- 'God also bearing witness both with signs and wonders, with various miracles, and gifts of the Holy Spirit, according to His own will' (Hebrews 2:4).

## Hope, Strength and Joy in our Hearts
- 'Hope does not put us to shame, because God's love has been poured out into our hearts through the Holy Spirit, who has been given to us' (Romans 5:5).
- 'I speak the truth in Christ – I am not lying, my conscience confirms it through the Holy Spirit' (Romans 9:1).
- 'The Kingdom of God is not a matter of eating and drinking, but of righteousness, peace and joy in the Holy Spirit' (Romans 14:17).
- 'I pray that out of His glorious riches He may strengthen you with power through His Spirit in your inner being' (Ephesians 3:16).

## Firstfruits of the Spirit
- 'Not only so, but we ourselves, who have the firstfruits of the Spirit, groan inwardly as we wait eagerly for our adoption to sonship, the redemption of our bodies' (Romans 8:23).
- 'If the ministry of death...was glorious, so that the children of Israel could not look steadily at the face of Moses because of the glory of his countenance, which glory was passing away, how will the ministry of the Spirit not be more glorious?' (2 Corinthians 3:7-8).

# Chapter Twenty-Three

## Revealing Self

"There is a throne of self in each of us," said a disciple of the Lord, "and how we fight, battle and rage to stay seated on that throne! The four revelations I received were: 1. That this throne exists. 2. That I sit on it. 3. That I must choose to allow the Holy Spirit to take me off this throne and put Christ there. 4. That to do this I must side with the Holy Spirit against my self."

The Holy Spirit cannot work in His fullness through a vessel that chooses to be unfit for His use. How can He work through us to glorify Jesus Christ when pride, selfishness, unforgiveness, slander, anger, lust, rage, backbiting and criticism have taken control of our souls? Would we like to live in a home where people constantly dumped their rubbish? Likewise, the Holy Spirit does not want to live in such a vessel. Is the problem sin or something deeper? "The spirit indeed is willing, but the flesh is weak" (Mark 14:38).

Oswald J. Smith wrote: 'No sooner have I dealt with sin than I am compelled to deal with self and so must you. God insists on having first place. Where then do you stand in relation to His will? Have you really surrendered all to Jesus Christ? Do you recognise Him alone as your Lord and Master? Are you willing to go, where He wants you to go, to do what He wants you to do, and to be what He wants you to be? Have you still a will of your own, or is God's will yours and is it your supreme delight to please Him? Who holds the reins of your life? Who controls your actions? In your choices and decisions, is God the dictator? Or are you? Are you sold out to Jesus Christ?'[1]

"When Jesus was baptised the Holy Spirit drove Him into the wilderness (Mark 1:12), and many of the prophets and apostles were led in a similar way," said a disciple of the Lord. "Those who want to live their lives in the Spirit will also be led that way. In the wilderness away from the world, its opinions and the influence of people – even good Christian people, the Holy Spirit breaks down self and our resistance to God. He strips us bare and we learn in that barren place, what has value and what is worthless. We die daily, as He exposes all the root of rebellion, self and ambition inside of us. We realise how we lived off the praise of others, their encouragement and how much we did in churches to be seen! The wilderness is a terrible place, but it is there we truly meet God!"

Rees Howells also found that after the Holy Spirit had dealt with specific sins, He moved on to deal with self, the true root of all sin.

When we have walked with the Holy Spirit for sometime, He will reveal that our problem is no longer so much open sin, but self. Our own self-interest will be revealed in its true ugliness and we learn that even the good things we thought we did for Christ, were actually birthed in self. The Pharisees were very religious and outwardly seemed like good people. They fasted, prayed and gave, but Jesus could see that all their religious devotion was to impress man, not God (Matthew 6:16, 9:14-15, 23:26, Luke 18:11-14).

'I am finding God's Word most precious,' wrote Oswald J. Smith in his diary: 'How it reveals the abominations of my heart! – Doubt, unbelief, spiritual pride, coldness, prayerlessness, powerlessness and indifference, as well as the awful abomination of the Church – the lack of separation, the worldliness of the membership, ungodly choirs, worldly methods of raising money, such as bazaars, concerts, entertainments etc., the failure to differentiate between the holy and profane, the clean and the unclean. Do we need a revival? God knows we do.'[2]

Rees Howells discovered that 'self must be released from itself to become the agent of the Holy Spirit. God first has to deal to the bottom with all that is natural. Love of money, personal ambition, natural affection for family and loved ones, the appetites of the body, the love of food and life itself, all that makes even a Christian live unto himself, for his own comfort or advantage, for his own advancement, even his own circle of friends has to go to the cross. It is no theoretical death, but a real crucifixion with Christ our Lord, such as only the Holy Spirit Himself can make actual in the experience of His servants. Paul's testimony must be made ours, "I have been and still am crucified with Christ." '

As Rees Howells submitted to the Holy Spirit His Teacher, who brought him closer to his Lord and Saviour, He would 'search his heart and throw light on his daily life, revealing any motives or actions that needed confession and cleansing. But the Spirit's dealings were not so much with outward shortcomings as with the self-nature out of which they sprang.'

When the Holy Spirit came to visit the Bible College that Rees Howells had founded in 1924, Wales, UK, He came not to bless people, but to possess them. 'In the light of His holiness, it was not so much sin we saw as self,' testified one of the staff. 'We saw pride and self-motives underlying everything we had ever done. Lust and self-pity were discovered in places where we had never suspected them, and we had to confess we knew nothing of the Holy Spirit as an indwelling Person. We knew our bodies should be the temples of the Holy Spirit but when He pressed the question, 'Who is living in your body?' We could not say that the Holy Spirit was. We would have done so once, but not now since we had seen Him.'

The Holy Spirit manifested Himself amongst them in such a way that they saw Him as God. 'In His nature He was just like Jesus Christ – He would never live for self, but always for others."

To deny the deep root of self, the Holy Spirit will lead us to the cross and ask us to crucify the sinful nature (Galatians 5:24). Jesus said, "Whoever desires to come after Me, let him deny himself and take up his cross, and follow Me" (Mark 8:34).

The Holy Spirit, if received in His fullness, will never allow us to live for self. 'The first step in real consecration is the dethronement of self,' wrote John George Govan, the founder of the Faith Mission, in Edinburgh, UK: 'Previously it was: "What I think," "what I said," etc. Though self is dethroned, the personality remains. Self does not die. Self has to be dethroned and then denied.'[3] The baptism of fire means the abandonment of the life lived for self and its desires, and in its place a life lived through the fire of God for His will alone.

"The greatest mistake committed Christians make in their spiritual lives is partial obedience," declared a disciple of the Lord. "After a time of blessing when we first meet the Lord, the first few steps in this new obedience will lead the Christian out of their Egypt of self and into the wilderness of testing. It is in the wilderness where we learn faith, perseverance and develop character (2 Peter 1:5-9). This is the route we all take; however, many Christians get so tired of the desert where self is revealed and crucified, that they give up obeying. This partial obedience means they never enter into the Promised Land. I have seen this time and time again. Countless numbers of Christians have stepped out in faith and then given up whilst still in the desert. They forget that the desert is always the route to the Promised Land!

"If I can give any advice to committed Christians it would be this: Practice total obedience, without leaving one thing undone and always persevere. If you do this, you will enter the Promised Land, and will in time come to understand that the Lord led you into the desert to take Egypt out of you. In the desert He reveals self – crucifies self and this develops the right character for living in the Promised Land. No-one can enter the Promised Land and still think like they did in Egypt!"

Missionary to India, Praying Hyde said, "Self must not only be dead, but buried out of sight, for the stench of the unburied self-life will frighten souls away from Jesus."

*Questions to consider:* Who sits on the throne of your heart? Do you honour self or crucify self?

*Actions:* Ask the Holy Spirit to open your eyes to your self nature. Then invite Him to fill that self with His Divine Presence.

# Chapter Twenty-Four

## Live According to the Spirit, Not the Flesh

- 'Therefore, there is now no condemnation for those who are in Christ Jesus, because through Christ Jesus the law of the Spirit who gives life has set you free from the law of sin and death' (Romans 8:1-2).
- 'Those who live according to the flesh have their minds set on what the flesh desires; but those who live in accordance with the Spirit have their minds set on what the Spirit desires' (Romans 8:5).
- 'You, however, are not in the realm of the flesh but are in the realm of the Spirit, if indeed the Spirit of God lives in you. And if anyone does not have the Spirit of Christ, they do not belong to Christ. But if Christ is in you, then even though your body is subject to death because of sin, the Spirit gives life because of righteousness. And if the Spirit of Him who raised Jesus from the dead is living in you, He who raised Christ from the dead will also give life to your mortal bodies because of His Spirit who lives in you' (Romans 8:9-11).
- 'For if you live according to the flesh, you will die; but if by the Spirit you put to death the misdeeds of the body, you will live. For those who are led by the Spirit of God are the children of God' (Romans 8:13-14).
- 'The Spirit you received does not make you slaves, so that you live in fear again; rather, the Spirit you received brought about your adoption to sonship. And by Him we cry, "Abba, Father." The Spirit Himself testifies with our spirit that we are God's children' (Romans 8:15-16).
- 'Walk in the Spirit and you shall not fulfil the lust of the flesh. For the flesh lusts against the Spirit and the Spirit against the flesh; and these are contrary to one another, so that you do not do the things that you wish. But if you are led by the Spirit, you are not under the law. Now the works of the flesh are evident, which are: adultery, fornication, uncleanness, lewdness, idolatry, sorcery, hatred, contentions, jealousies, outbursts of wrath, selfish ambitions…but the fruit of the Spirit is love, joy, peace, longsuffering, kindness, goodness, faithfulness, gentleness, self-control…if we live in the Spirit, let us also walk in the Spirit' (Galatians 5:16-25).

# Chapter Twenty-Five

## Surrender To Christ

Imagine yourself stood in front of a wall, twenty-four feet high and twelve feet thick. On the other side of that wall is the pathway to the full destiny and purpose of God for your life (Ephesians 2:10). Beyond this enormous barrier hang the keys to your victory, liberty and ability to walk closely with God. After years of standing in front of this wall, waiting for God to do something to smash it down, you begin to fast and plead with God to break it down. You seek counsel from others, read Christian books, listen to preachers, rebuke Satan and attempt with all your strength to smash the wall down. Then after years of failure, lost hope and spiritual stagnation, you cry out in exhaustion, "Lord, please help me break through this wall." Then, one day when you are quiet in the presence of God, the Holy Spirit whispers to you, "The wall is self." Stunned into silence, you begin to realise that every time the Holy Spirit spoke to you in the past you disobeyed! The wall is not Satan, but your disobedience. "If you fully lay down self," the Holy Spirit says, "the wall will fall."

When we were born again, we were convicted and sealed by the Holy Spirit. Afterwards, we can be baptised in the Holy Spirit. Yet all of this is still an introduction to the Person of the Holy Spirit; it is like shaking hands for the first time and saying, "Hello." Now we must ask ourselves – do we want to get to know the Person of the Spirit?

If we are to invite Him into our lives in a deeper way, we must first make room for Him. So far, His life has filled parts of our lives – as we have step by step made room for Him to live and work within us; but if we are to go through – He needs all of us. To move forward we are shown the pathway of full surrender to God's will and are urged to invite the Holy Spirit in, not to bless us, but to possess every area of our being! We are shown the opportunity of laying down everything and having no further claim on our lives. The thought is daunting, yet everything He has done in our lives so far has been preparing us for this!

Stephen Crisp, a preacher from the 1600s acknowledged that full Lordship is what God really wants from us all: "If a man hopes to be saved by Christ, he must be ruled by Him," he said. "It is contrary to all manner of reason that the devil should rule a man and Christ be his Saviour."[1]

Many Christians want to be saved by the Lord Jesus Christ and have a desire to be used by God, but sadly they refuse to lay down their lives, to be completely obedient to Him. Christians often live in a world of contradictions, where Jesus is acknowledged as Saviour, but refuted as Lord. How strange it is to believe that Jesus is God and by His sacrifice we are saved, and yet at the same time refuse to heed anything He says to us! (Luke 6:46).

Jesus said, "Whoever desires to come after Me, let him deny himself and take up his cross, and follow Me. For whoever desires to save his life will lose it, but whoever loses his life for My sake and the gospel's will save it" (Mark 8:34-35).

The partial obedience of Christians leads to inner guilt and there is a danger that to pacify these feelings believers start to 'do works' for Christ, in which they are still completely in control. In 1932, Earnest C.W. Boulton refuted a life of sacrifice without obedience: 'God does not want our work, but He does want our will,' he wrote. 'When we give it, we give all; when we withhold it, we give nothing.'[2]

Our resistance by not allowing the Holy Spirit to live in and through us, to glorify God, is the manifestation of the old flesh life or carnal nature fighting for survival. We want God to speak to us and to do wonderful things, but we also want a vote on His direction! But we cannot be led of the Spirit of God, whilst we remain in the valley of decision: 'Multitudes, multitudes in the valley of decision!' (Joel 3:14). Until we have finally decided to surrender all to Jesus Christ, and to obey unconditionally the will and purposes of the Holy Spirit, there is no reason why He should speak to us! God does not need a democratic council to debate His will and vote on it. He needs empty vessels who will obey Him!

"For many years I have witnessed Christians attempting to serve God," said a disciple of the Lord. "They give up so much to attend Bible College, or to serve in a ministry, or to be faithful in their places of work – yet they do not give up the throne of self within. Therefore the Lord tries to lead them and they partially obey Him. Partial obedience brings the same results as disobedience!

"The great problem with partial obedience is you cannot end up at the final destination by partially following the path. Sometimes I think our lives with God are like getting on a train across a vast region. If you delay getting on the train and wait for the second, third or fourth train, you will only make it part way to the destination you were called to. Also, if you get on the first train and get off to do some sight-seeing in the world, you may get back on the second or third train etc., but you will miss all the right connections.

"There are many believers who have stepped out in faith and onto the right train, at the right time and began to travel into God's will. However, when trouble, trials or discouragements came, they transferred to another, to a separate line and ended up criss-crossing the region and going backwards, etc.

"The Israelites left Egypt and spent forty years trying to make an eleven day journey! (Deuteronomy 1:2). Many do the same today. There is only one remedy to travelling in the wrong direction and that is to abdicate as the driver. Yes abdicate! Remove yourself from the inner throne of self, give Christ the Lordship of your life and obey the Spirit of Christ in all things (1 Peter 1:11). Even if you have got onto the wrong train and are heading in the wrong direction, He can pick you up in the Spirit and set you where you should be. Never underestimate the power of God to restore the years the locusts have eaten" (Joel 2:25).

Until we have made up our minds to surrender all to the Lord Jesus Christ, and invite the Holy Spirit to come and live His life in and through us – all our praying, testifying and desire to hear from God is a shambles. How can God use us if we are not truly His? How can we be filled with the fullness of God, if we are filled with self? How can we be channels of God, if we are still channelling so much of the world, the flesh and the devil? Why would He speak to us if He already knows we will not obey?

Rees Howells faced these startling facts as a young man and realised that it would cost him everything to obey the Holy Spirit unconditionally. "Once you are God's channel," he said, "on no account can you disobey Him, or bring in your own ideas."

The Holy Spirit showed Rees Howells the cost of full surrender and it shook him. "I saw the Holy Spirit as a Person apart from flesh and blood, and He made it very plain that He would never share my life. I saw the honour He gave me in offering to indwell me, but there were many things very dear to me, and I knew He wouldn't keep one of them. The change He would make was very clear. It meant every bit of my fallen nature was to go to the cross, and He would bring in His own life and His own nature."

Rees Howells knew that the Lord was asking him for unconditional surrender and once this is done with all sincerity, it is done for ever, for it is a great sin to make a vow and then reevaluate (Matthew 5:37). "I had received a sentence of death!" Rees Howells testified, "who could give his life up to another person? One thing He reminded me of, was that He had only come to take what I had already promised the Saviour, not in part, but the whole. I saw that only the Holy Spirit in me could live like Christ. He was not going to take any superficial surrender. He was to put His finger on each part of my self life, and I had to decide in cold blood. He could never take a thing away until I gave my consent."

Rees Howells was raised in a sheltered community in Wales, UK, where a conservative Christian moral culture was the foundation of all. Even for non-Christians, breaking the Sabbath was uncommon and before he was born again, Rees was concerned that attending a football match could be sin. Bearing all this in mind, when the Holy Spirit entered, Rees Howells said, "He was coming in as God, and I had lived as man and He told me, 'What is permissible to an ordinary man will not be permissible to you.' "

Rees Howells had to accept the implications of full surrender. He could not love money, choose his own career, marry whoever he wanted, or live where he wanted – his life would never be his own again. All his personal ambitions would need to be crucified, and just like the men of God in the Bible, his reputation would have to die also (Hebrews 13:13). The Holy Spirit summarised full surrender for him: "On no account will I allow you to cherish a single thought of self, and the life I will live in you will be one hundred percent for others. You will never be able to save yourself, any more than Christ could when He was on earth. Now, are you willing?"

Rees Howells followed the Lord into this life of full surrender and witnessed the power of God move spiritual mountains, in healing, revival and in supernatural provision. Then, many years later he presented the same challenge and cost of full surrender to all those who listened to him at the Bible College he founded in Wales. As each person considered the cost, the Holy Spirit came to meet with them. "One by one the Holy Spirit met with us," said one staff member. "We broke in tears and contrition before Him. From one after another rose the cry as it did from Isaiah, when he too 'saw the Lord,' and said, 'Woe is me for I am undone...unclean' (Isaiah 6:5). One by one our wills were broken and we yielded to His unconditional terms. As we gave ourselves to Him, to each there came the glorious realisation – the Spirit of God had entered into our vessels and the wonder of our privilege just overwhelmed us."

'Like others who have willed themselves unreservedly and irrevocably to God, Hudson Taylor proved how much the Divine hand can accomplish in one life and ministry,' wrote Earnest C.W. Boulton in 1932. 'Let us never forget that if we give ourselves to God in this wholehearted manner, God gives Himself back to us in fullest measure. It is only as we let ourselves go – literally throw ourselves upon God's will, that He can meet us in the floodtide fullness; and only then can we prove the exhilarating and exultant joy of being utterly lost in God; carried captive in the Spirit to the heights and depths of Divine impartation and impregnation. As long as we so tenaciously cling to our own tiny resources, so long shall we remain but ankle-deep in spiritual experiences. So many are content to wade when God's plan is that we should swim.'[3]

Healing evangelist, F.F. Bosworth wrote in 1924: 'God's work of quickening or increasing the Divine life in our spirit, soul and body is hindered or limited when we are anything less than *full* of the Spirit. Jesus said that He came, not only that we might have life, but that we might have it more abundantly.'[4]

In the 1940s, the Hebridean revivalist Duncan Campbell was speaking on Elijah building the Lord's altar, as he challenged the nation of Israel to reject the prophets of Baal (1 Kings 18:31-40). Campbell imagined that Elijah was waiting for the fire of God to fall, but there was still one last piece of the sacrifice that was not on the altar. It was only a very small part of the sacrifice, but for some reason, Campbell indicated, it was not on the altar. Campbell explained we all must examine our own hearts and ask ourselves if we too are holding back something from the altar of sacrifice. It may be something small and seemly insignificant, but that tiny thing which we withhold from God, is the very thing which stops the fire of God falling in our lives. He concluded, "If you are not prepared to bring the 'last piece' to the altar, all your praying is but the laughing-stock of devils. It is about time that we got into the grips of reality. Can you say today, 'God, you've got the last piece?'"

Christians are often fearful of the idea of full surrender to Christ, but we must ask ourselves: Is my future in safer hands when I am in control, or when God is in control? (Romans 8:28). Can I trust the Holy Spirit to make better decisions about my future, than I can? Do I believe that the Prince of Peace, who 'told us these things that our joy may be fulfilled,' can lead me into a life where my peace, provision and joy are found in Him?

The Holy Spirit can only fill and guide our lives, with the measure that we surrender to Him, and Christ is only Lord of what we give to Him. The baptism of fire can only descend upon us when the altar is fully made and our life is laid upon it, waiting for God's fire to fall. J. Edwin Orr, the revivalist and revival historian wrote: 'If you want to serve God, "Present your body a living sacrifice, holy, acceptable to God" – it is your reasonable service (Romans 12:1). Jesus said, "Why call Me, 'Lord, Lord,' and do not do the things I say?" (Luke 6:46). He does not want the lip-service of sentimental humbug; He wants the heart service of reasonable honesty. What is more, He needs it. "My son, give me thy heart..." (Proverbs 23:26). If the Law required us to love the Lord with all our heart, we should not withhold it under grace. Full surrender is our reasonable service because "the love of Christ compels us" ' (2 Corinthians 5:14).[5]

We learn in the Bible that we can only prove what the perfect will of God for our lives is, when we meet the conditions found in the book of Romans: 'Present your bodies a living sacrifice, holy, acceptable to God...and do not be conformed to this world, but be transformed by the renewing of your mind, that you may prove what is that good, acceptable and perfect will of God' (Romans 12:1-2). If you want the full will of God for your life, you must pay the full price!

"Placing my life on the Lord's altar was a scary thought," said a disciple of the Lord. "It's not easy to give up the rights to my one and only life. Yet, bit by bit I placed more of my life on the altar of God, and allowed His fire to come down and consume the sacrifice of My life. The fire of the Lord was painful, and I learnt that before

He can resurrect the ashes of any sacrifice, the fire must fall. At some points it seems like all I had was ash! God is the great Vinedresser and when He found branches in my life that did not bear fruit, or branches which drew away strength from fruit bearing, He pruned them. Jesus explained this process in John 15.

"As time went on, I found myself bearing more fruit and I had my spiritual eyes opened. I could finally see that the 'dead wood' in my life was no good to me, to others or to God. It had to be pruned, so I could grow into the will of God.

"As the years passed, I watched as the Lord honoured my willingness to surrender to His pruning, and He opened my eyes again. I realised that everyone on earth is building an 'altar' to something and are 'sacrificing' their lives on their altars. All are laying down their lives on the altar of their wants and perceived needs.

"Many wanted to be married outside of the will of God or earn vast sums of money, so they could own luxury items. Many wanted positions in the church so they could be seen, and the more they wanted, the more they had to give up and sacrifice. I saw this in many people's lives and many gave up so much, for so little. They are paying the price for the sacrifices they made on their altar to 'self,' and there is no heavenly reward for giving up your life for what you want. However, for those who give up everything for the Lord, there are rewards in this life and for all eternity (Mark 10:29-31).

"When all is said and done, we all lay everything on one altar or another. We all leave this world with nothing. The only things that leave earth and get to eternity are souls. What we did with the talents and gifts God gave us is our choice and we shall only be rewarded for what we did for Him, not what we did for ourselves and our wants (Matthew 25:15-28). If we spend all our gifts and talents to get items, or positions of power in society, then God have mercy on us on the Day of Judgment. He did not give us gifts to waste on our own wants and desires (James 4:3). This is all selfish in nature."

*Questions to consider:* Have you surrendered everything to the Lord? Is Jesus Christ the true Lord of your life? Can you honestly say Jesus is Lord? Have you been crucified with Christ? Can you honestly say you no longer live and Christ lives in you?

*Actions:* Spend some time to consider the cost of full surrender. Ask God to make you 'willing to be made willing' to surrender all, just as Rees Howells and many others had to.

# Chapter Twenty-Six

## Heed the Spirit

- 'In reading this, then, you will be able to understand my insight into the mystery of Christ, which was not made known to people in other generations as it has now been revealed by the Spirit to God's holy apostles and prophets. This mystery is that through the gospel the Gentiles are heirs together with Israel, members together of one body, and sharers together in the promise in Christ Jesus' (Ephesians 3:4-6).
- 'This is what we speak, not in words taught us by human wisdom but in words taught by the Spirit, explaining spiritual realities with Spirit taught words' (1 Corinthians 12:13).
- 'Therefore, as the Holy Spirit says, "Today, if you will hear His voice..." ' (Hebrews 3:7).
- 'The Holy Spirit indicating this, that the way into the Holiest of All was not yet made manifest while the first tabernacle was still standing' (Hebrews 9:8).
- 'But the Holy Spirit also witnesses to us; for after He had said before, "This is the covenant that I will make with them after those days, says the Lord: I will put My laws into their hearts, and in their minds I will write them" ' (Hebrews 10:15-16).
- Jesus said, "Whoever has ears, let them hear what the Spirit says to the churches" (Revelation 2:7).
- Jesus said, "Whoever has ears, let them hear what the Spirit says to the churches" (Revelation 2:17).
- Jesus said, "Whoever has ears, let them hear what the Spirit says to the churches" (Revelation 2:29).
- Jesus said, "Whoever has ears, let them hear what the Spirit says to the churches" (Revelation 3:6).
- Jesus said, "Whoever has ears, let them hear what the Spirit says to the churches" (Revelation 3:13).
- Jesus said, "Whoever has ears, let them hear what the Spirit says to the churches" (Revelation 3:22).
- 'I heard a voice from heaven say, "Write this: Blessed are the dead who die in the Lord from now on." "Yes," says the Spirit, "they will rest from their labour, for their deeds will follow them" ' (Revelation 14:13).
- 'He carried me away in the Spirit to a mountain great and high' (Revelation 21:10).

# Chapter Twenty-Seven

## Possessed by the Holy Spirit

The Hebridean revivalist Duncan Campbell once spoke of seeing, "God in dungarees," working in a field. The congregation were confused – did He see God dressed as a man? Campbell went on to explain that he saw a man, so filled with God that he lost sight of the man and saw God in him. Has anyone ever looked into your eyes and seen the unending love of God, the mercy of Christ or God's holy indignation? What a challenge!

When we study the Bible carefully we find there are several distinct stages of blessing and infilling that men and women of God have experienced with the Holy Spirit. All these opportunities are given to all who will choose to pay the price to go deeper with the Holy Spirit.

1. Conviction leading to repentance and faith, followed by receiving the seal of the Holy Spirit (John 20:22, Ephesians 1:13).

2. The baptism of the Holy Spirit (Acts 2:1-4).

3. Continually receiving more of the Holy Spirit (Acts 4:29-31).

4. Possessed or filled with the fullness of God (Judges 6:34, 2 Chronicles 24:2, Ezekiel 2:2, 3:24, Ephesians 3:19). The phrase 'possession' or 'possessed' by the Holy Spirit is used in various translations of the Bible in several Old Testament verses. This means living a life continually baptised in the fire of God.

Before we consider this in-depth, it is important to recognise that every believer is on a journey with Christ. We cannot divide believers into the four categories above and guess who belongs in which section! We can only judge self and humble ourselves before God.

The opposite to humility is pride and it was pride that kept the religious leaders in Jesus' day from His message; they already knew and had everything! They thought they were so right with God that they were unwilling to receive anything more from God, and were unable to recognise the Messiah when He stood before them! 'The Pharisees and lawyers rejected the will of God for themselves, not having been baptised by him' (Luke 7:30). That religious spirit tries to cling onto Christians today, so if you find yourself holding your nose up and your mind resisting any new revelation from God, humble yourself for your own good and repent (Proverbs 29:1).

In the New Testament we learn that the disciples had many opportunities and experiences to receive anew from the Holy Spirit, and this also applies to us. The disciples were converted in John 20:22, when Jesus breathed on them and said, "Receive the Holy

Spirit." This was when they were quickened and sealed by the Holy Spirit (Ephesians 4:30). Later in Acts 2:1-4, they were baptised in the Holy Spirit. However, many of them found there were further areas of themselves to be surrendered to the Lord, to allow the Holy Spirit to replace self, with Himself. In Acts 2 they received tongues of fire and spoke the word, which led to problems with the authorities. In Acts 4:29-31, the boldness of the Holy Spirit came upon them and filled their weaknesses.

Having experienced new revelations of the Holy Spirit, Paul wrote that believers should, 'keep on being filled constantly and continually,' as the original Greek reveals. As the years progressed many sought the Spirit to teach them and fill areas of themselves that were stilled filled with self. Paul knew about this and wrote about a total infilling – to be 'filled with all the fullness of God' (Ephesians 3:19). This includes giving oneself fully and totally to God, and allowing Him to fill every area.

It is the same in our lives. After the Holy Spirit has convicted us of sin and we respond with faith in Christ, we are sealed with the Holy Spirit (Ephesians 1:13). We are saved, but not baptised or filled with the Spirit. Paul explains that the seal of the Spirit is the revelation that we are a part of God's family. 'For by one Spirit we were all baptised into one body – whether Jews or Greeks, whether slaves or free and have all been made to drink into one Spirit' (1 Corinthians 12:13). We are then saved, but not empowered.

Paul experienced the sealing of the Spirit when he was saved (Acts 9:1-6). However, he was not baptised in the Holy Spirit and for this reason Jesus Himself directed him to his need (Acts 9:6). Three days after Paul was saved and received the seal of the Spirit, He had a further experience with God and was baptised in the Holy Spirit (Acts 9:9, 17). However, this was not the end for Paul, for he had many more experiences with God. Paul later explained that Christians should not be drunk with wine, because they need to be continually filled with the Spirit of God (Ephesians 5:19). Therefore, he was first sealed, then baptised, and then he continually sought to be renewed and filled with the Spirit. Finally, Paul wrote of 'being filled with the fullness of God' (Ephesians 3:19). This was more than being blessed by God's Spirit, washed over, or anointed – Paul spoke of being completely filled with the fullness of God. This is what some Christian leaders call being 'possessed by the Spirit' (Judges 6:34, 2 Chronicles 24:2, Ezekiel 2:2, 3:24).

The phrase 'possessed by the Holy Spirit' is not common today, however at the beginning of the twentieth century, as the Holy Spirit was being poured out anew in the Church, many of the prominent ministers of that day preached about being 'possessed by the Holy Spirit.'

In Britain, some of the most influential preachers of the day made this phrase common, and for the following seventy years, people influenced by those ministers preached, wrote books and taught others that there is more all can experience in God.

In the 1962 book *I Believe in the Holy Ghost,* Maynard James wrote: 'Before there can be the outflow of Divine power from our lives there must be the incoming of the Holy Spirit to possess the deepest recesses of our being.'[1] The book was endorsed by Dr. Martyn Lloyd-Jones, Duncan Campbell, Norman Grubb and many other famous Christian leaders. Rees Howells and his son Samuel invited many prominent and well respected preachers to the Every Creature Conferences in Wales from 1936-1964. Rees and Samuel Howells constantly preached on the need to be 'possessed by the Holy Spirit' and these messages were echoed by many others.

In the context of this book, the phrase 'possessed by the Holy Spirit' is used to explain that there is something far deeper than the baptism of the Spirit. This is the 'fire' that John the Baptist preached on and it is being 'filled with the fullness of God' (Ephesians 3:19).

Jesus Christ was the first to receive the Spirit 'without measure' (John 3:34), and when Jesus taught on the promise of the Holy Spirit He said, "How much more will your heavenly Father give the Holy Spirit to those that ask Him?" (Luke 11:13). The phrase, "How much more," indicates the willingness of God to go far beyond all we have experienced. Many have been baptised in the Holy Spirit, but have never experienced the fire. The fire is the next step. "I indeed baptise you with water unto repentance, but He who is coming after me is mightier than I, whose sandals I am not worthy to carry. He will baptise you with the Holy Spirit and fire" (Matthew 3:11).

The promise of the fullness of the Holy Spirit has been recorded throughout the Scriptures: "My people...I will put My Spirit within you" (Ezekiel 37:13-14). The Church is familiar with the concept of demonic possession, as demonic powers take full control of a person against his or her will. Yet, we are often unfamiliar with the biblical concept of the Holy Spirit taking full possession of a willing individual for His purposes. When the Holy Spirit takes full possession, the individual chooses to lay down his or her own free will on the altar of sacrifice, and the Holy Spirit then lives His life through this empty vessel. In everyday, through every moment the new 'vessel' sides with the Spirit against self and its will. The personality of the individual does not disappear; but he or she no longer sits on the throne of self, as he or she gives way to Christ.

"God wants your life, your hands, your feet. God wants your heart," said the evangelist John R. Rice in 1946, as he preached on the fullness of the Spirit. "God wants self on the altar. He wants self made over, and anointed and endued so that you can be a soul winner. Are you filled with the Holy Spirit in the Bible sense? Do you really believe you have what Bible Christians had? Do you have what John the Baptist had when he was filled with the Holy Ghost, so that many people of Israel turned to the Lord their God? Do you have what Barnabas had? He was a good man, full of faith and the Holy Ghost, and people were added to the Lord as a result of Barnabas' ministry. Do you have that? Do you have what dying Stephen had? He was full of the Holy Ghost and faith. Do you have, I ask, what these Bible preachers and Bible laymen and Bible women had? And the power – why, it spread like wildfire, and Jerusalem was turned 'upside down.' That is what they said, 'Ye have filled Jerusalem with your doctrine,' and that Paul 'turned the world upside down.' I wonder, do you fill Jerusalem with your doctrine and turn the world upside down as they did? Our trouble is primarily with the people of God – our sinful carelessness, our powerlessness…I wonder whether you are satisfied to go on never filled with the Holy Ghost?"[2]

"We hear a lot of preaching on the Holy Spirit in some circles of the modern Church," said a disciple of the Lord, "but the message being preached today is very different from what used to be preached. Today we come to be blessed by God, but in the past they came to be possessed by God. Today we come to get 'stuff' from God, but in the past they came to lay down their all for God. Today we come to be healed, but in the past they gave up their lives so God could heal the world through them. In the past people came to the altar to lay something down, but now were supposed to come forward to receive something new.

"Because we don't meet the Spirit of God on the same conditions as our forefathers, He in turn does not meet us like He met them. We are blessed, but afterward we do not obey. The Bible states we should 'walk in the Spirit' (Galatians 5:16), yet as soon as we get out of God's house, we begin to walk in the flesh again. We set our minds on what we want, need or feel, and the Spirit is grieved. Where are the men and women of the Spirit?

"I have travelled to ministries where great men and women of God used to live and work, and I have often been disappointed by what I have found. The legacy of such people is not physical, but spiritual. Perhaps I was looking for the anointing to abide on the new staff or on the land, but the living water always remains with the Lord. He is the source of the living water, and until the new generation of staff pays the full price in God's currency of unconditional surrender of the body, mind and will to the Lord, they will merely be stewards of the ministry. The only way any person can receive the same anointing of the Holy Spirit as these great men and women of God did, is to pay the same price!

"I have found that people are often trying to catch the anointing, recover it from the past or dig it up. There is some truth to all such experiences; however you can never receive the Holy Spirit on the cheap. You have to pay the full price. You cannot bargain with Him. He will not strive with us forever. He will not spend His time fighting against our will, our rebellion and our disobedience. We cannot expect to give Him one percent of our lives and expect to walk in the same anointing as Elijah. This prophet's successor had to pay the same price as his predecessor and so must we."

'We speak of the Holy Spirit as a gift of God to the believer in Christ,' wrote missionary to Tibet, Geoffrey T. Bull in 1955. 'It is not so much our possessing the Spirit, as the Spirit possessing us. On acceptance of Christ the believer is born of the Spirit, yet it may be but slowly that He will obtain full sovereignty of the heart and will.' [3]

In the 1930s, Rees Howells taught his staff to allow the Spirit to enter and take full possession. They had all lived sacrificial Christian lives for many years, but the Holy Spirit showed them, "There is all the difference in the world between your surrendered life in My hands and I living My life in your body." When they considered the cost, they realised that the Spirit never lives for self, but for the will and purposes of God the Father. Therefore, if they responded, He would lead them into a deeper life of crucifixion, in order for Christ's resurrection to be manifested through them. 'Who then is willing to consecrate himself this day to the Lord?' (1 Chronicles 29:5).

It is important to understand that when we invite the Holy Spirit into our lives to possess every area of our being, we are not immediately transformed into the image of Christ. Full surrender to the Holy Spirit means giving Him the right to take any areas of our lives and crucify them, so the image of Christ can be expressed through us. This is an ongoing process that never finishes. Only the Holy Spirit can lead us through this process of being transformed into the image of Christ. We 'are being transformed into the same image from glory to glory, just as by the Spirit of the Lord' (2 Corinthians 3:18).

Before we give ourselves totally to the Holy Spirit we can play at being changed from within, but the Holy Spirit will not play at being a Christian. He will transform us from glory to glory, to be more like Christ. Rees Howells called this 'confronting all unreality' in his life. "A soul cannot be sure of Divine guidance unless possessed by the Holy Spirit," said the Rev. Evan Hopkins, "when yielded up to the Holy Spirit, He guides, but it costs us our will."[4]

When the Holy Spirit came to the College founded by Rees Howells, one of the staff explained, "He made it clear that He was not asking for service, but for a sacrifice. Our God is a consuming fire and if God the Holy Spirit was to take possession of these bodies, then His life was going to consume all that there was of ours. We had often sung, 'I want to be like Jesus,' but when we had the offer from the Person of the Holy Spirit, who is just like the Saviour to come and live that life daily and hourly in us, we found how unreal we had been. How much there was in us that still wanted to live our own lives – that shrank from this 'sentence of death!' We now began to see the meaning of Christ's words – 'For whoever desires to save his life will lose it, but whoever loses his life for My sake will save it' " (Luke 9:24).

One by one, the staff at the College surrendered their lives to the Lord and welcomed the Holy Spirit to enter them, not to bless, but to live His life in them. Their testimonies explained how they entered this deeper life in Christ. "But now He had come and we were out of it. The Holy Spirit told us, 'I have not come to give you peace, joy or victory. I have not come to give you any temporal blessing at all. You will find all that you need in the Saviour, Jesus Christ. But I have come to put you to the cross, so that I may live in your body for the sake of a lost world.' Then the Holy Spirit flooded into them and they were changed! "The personal experience was great and we became new people in Christ. The Bible became new. So often we had had to water down the Word to the level of our experience. But now the Person in us would insist on bringing our experience up to the level of His Word."

Together Rees Howells and his team learnt that no-one can say in truth, "Jesus is Lord," except by the Holy Spirit (1 Corinthians 12:3), and they were experiencing what Andrew Murray wrote about: 'Just as water ever seeks and fills the lowest place, so the moment God finds you abased and empty, His glory and power flows in.'

Too often Christians spend their lives in an inward battle, fighting and resisting the perfect will of God for their lives. Many have not fulfilled the command of Romans 12:1, to lay down their lives completely on God's altar. Their whole Christian experience is a tug-of-war, as God pulls them one way, and the flesh, the world and the devil pulls in the opposite direction. As human will is the ultimate decider in this battle, man will constantly side with self. This is why Rees Howells explained that we must side with the Holy Spirit against self. When the Holy Spirit comes in to take possession of a body, He comes to live His life without contention – without fights, without strife, and He does not give us a vote on God's will! He comes to live His life and our lives must go.

"The Holy Spirit waits to pour His life and fullness, transforming the whole being and calling forth the things of joy and beauty once more," said Frederick A. Tatford, at Westminster Chapel in London, in 1946. "Such an experience is not free of cost, however. There is a price to pay – the price of complete self-abandonment to God."[5]

Duncan Campbell said, "If the fire is to fall the last piece must be handled." Every last bit of self must be placed on the altar before He will come in and take full possession. "The truth about the Holy Spirit is discoverable and verifiable only by submission to His power," he preached. "We may talk about Him, we may think about Him, but only when we submit can we know His mighty power."[6]

People that have been blessed by the Holy Spirit and want more, will ever be seeking after new experiences and the next blessing, but the Christian who has surrendered all to the Holy Spirit and welcomed Him in all His fullness, will not need to keep searching, because the Spirit will come to abide. He will come to be the Teacher and Guide into the will of God (John 14:26).

There can be some confusion about the work and ministry of the Spirit in the life of the believer, but they can be simplified by stating: We can be sealed, baptised and filled. He can come upon, clothe us with power and fall on us. What does the Bible say? The Holy Spirit can seal us for salvation (John 20:22, Romans 8:9-11, 1 Corinthians 6:19, 12:13). We can be baptised in the Spirit (Matthew 3:11, Acts 10:45-46, 11:16). The Holy Spirit can come on us and clothe with power (Luke 24:49, Acts 1:8). We can be filled with the Spirit (Acts 2, 9:17). The Holy Spirit can be outpoured (Joel 2:28-29, Acts 2:17-18, 2:33, 10:45), and the Spirit can fall upon us (Acts 8:16, 10:44). There is more!

"Many have been blessed by the Holy Spirit," said a disciple of the Lord, "and yet they know there is much more; just like the disciples found (John 20:22, Acts 2:17-18). What these people need is to be baptised into Christ's death, so the resurrected Christ can be raised in them (Romans 6:3). As their lives are crucified, the life of Christ can flood in.

"The great Christians of the past are remembered as such because they gave up their lives and let God live through them. As the Bible states: 'That I may know Him and the power of His resurrection and the fellowship of His sufferings, being conformed to His death' (Philippians 3:10). Like Paul, these people crucified their ambitions, wills and desires, so God's will and purposes could be manifested through them. Their greatness was in their surrender. As they surrendered, so they were filled. They were not great, it was Christ's greatness in them."

*Questions to consider:* Have you invited the Holy Spirit to enter into you and live His life? Are you prepared to become an empty vessel in order for Him to live His life through you?

*Actions:* Put the last piece of your sacrifice on the altar and invite the Holy Spirit to come in and possess you.

# Chapter Twenty-Eight

## Holy is the Lord

- 'Or do you not know that wrongdoers will not inherit the Kingdom of God? Do not be deceived: Neither the sexually immoral, nor idolaters, nor adulterers, nor men who have sex with men, nor thieves, nor the greedy, nor drunkards, nor slanderers, nor swindlers will inherit the Kingdom of God. And that is what some of you were. But you were washed, you were sanctified, you were justified in the name of the Lord Jesus Christ and by the Spirit of our God' (1 Corinthians 6:9-11).
- 'Do you not know that your bodies are temples of the Holy Spirit, who is in you, whom you have received from God? You are not your own' (1 Corinthians 6:19).
- 'Do not grieve the Holy Spirit of God, with whom you were sealed for the day of redemption. Get rid of all bitterness, rage and anger, brawling and slander, along with every form of malice. Be kind and compassionate to one another, forgiving each other, just as in Christ, God forgave you' (Ephesians 4:30-32).
- 'But fornication and all uncleanness or covetousness, let it not even be named among you, as is fitting for saints...For this you know that no fornicator, unclean person, nor covetous man, who is an idolater, has any inheritance in the Kingdom of Christ and God. Let no one deceive you with empty words, for because of these things the wrath of God comes upon the sons of disobedience. Therefore do not be partakers with them. For you were once darkness, but now you are light in the Lord. Walk as children of light, for the fruit of the Spirit is in all goodness, righteousness and truth (Ephesians 5:3-9).
- 'Do not be drunk with wine, in which is dissipation; but be filled with the Spirit, speaking to one another in psalms and hymns and spiritual songs, singing and making melody in your heart to the Lord' (Ephesians 5:18-19).
- Jesus said, "Repent or else I will come to you quickly and will fight against them with the sword of My mouth. He who has an ear, let him hear what the Spirit says to the churches. To him who overcomes I will give some of the hidden manna to eat. And I will give him a white stone and on the stone a new name written which no one knows except him who receives it" (Revelation 2:16-17).

# Chapter Twenty-Nine

## Him Living His Life

When we have surrendered all to the Lord and welcomed the Holy Spirit to live His life through us, there can be no more conflict with God over obedience. The Bible explains that faith in Christ saves us (Ephesians 2:8-10), and James explains that our obedience to God (John 14:15) is the proof we are saved: 'For as the body without the spirit is dead so faith without works is dead' (James 2:26).

Complete surrender and possession by the Holy Spirit means we have laid down our rights to protest, question and doubt Him. We will still need the gift of discernment to keep us in the light, but through our obedience we will witness the Holy Spirit beginning to reach out to the world through us. He will direct us to give to others, witness, pray and will lead us down unusual paths in order for Him to minister to the world through us. These outward manifestations of power will be encouraging, but He may also lead us into the hidden life of prayer, secret obedience and intercession, just as many of the prophets were.

During these experiences we learn that we are not the master of our own destiny, but we are stewards of the life Christ has given us. We learn that we do not own anything because He is the owner of all. We become His stewards in every area of our lives and this experience can never lead to any pride in our lives, as if we have done something special – because it is a small thing to give back to the God the very gifts He has given to us.

Jesus said, "So likewise you, when you have done all those things which you are commanded, say, 'We are unprofitable servants. We have done what was our duty to do' " (Luke 17:10). The Psalmist made the point that our lives are never our own, because it is God's breath that gives us life, and as He can withdraw His extension of life from us at anytime; our lives are already His (Psalm 104:29). We are the stewards of His breath, the time He gives us and His gifts.

C.S. Lewis thinking similar thoughts concluded: 'Does it not make a great difference whether I am, so to speak, the landlord of my own mind and body, or only a tenant, responsible to the real landlord? If somebody else made me, for His own purposes, then I shall have a lot of duties which I should not have if I simply belonged to myself.'[1]

When we give our lives and bodies back to God, for Him to live in and through us, we are only giving His gifts back to Him. C.S. Lewis summarised: 'Every faculty you have, your power of thinking or of moving your limbs from moment to moment, is given you by God. If you devoted every moment of your whole life exclusively to His service you could not give Him anything that was not in a sense His own already. So that when we talk of a man doing anything for God or giving anything to God, I will tell you what it is really like. It is like a small child going to its father and saying, "Daddy, give me sixpence to buy you a birthday present." Of course, the father does, and he is pleased with the child's present. It is all very nice and proper, but only a fool would think that the father is sixpence to the good on the transaction. When a man has made these two discoveries God can really get to work. It is after this that real life begins. The man is awake now.'[2]

One of the discoveries we learn when we finally lay down and surrender our lives to the Lord, is that we have been struggling and striving in the flesh all our Christian lives to 'do things for God.' Paul warned of the danger of 'trying to serve God,' without the direct leading of the Spirit. 'Now if anyone builds on this foundation with gold, silver, precious stones, wood, hay, straw, each one's work will become clear; for the Day will declare it, because it will be revealed by fire; and the fire will test each one's work, of what sort it is. If anyone's work which he has built on it endures, he will receive a reward. If anyone's work is burned, he will suffer loss; but he himself will be saved, yet so as through fire' (1 Corinthians 3:12-15).

However, there is also the danger of beginning in the Spirit, but then veering off into the flesh. There are many who have been called by God who made the first steps into their call, as they began by the Spirit's leading, but then something changed in them and what began by the Spirit was hijacked by human ability. They begin to seek advisors, plan strategies and trust in the counsel of men, instead of the counsel of the Spirit. This takes place when people are called by the Spirit, but do not become people of the Spirit.

There is a great danger that those who have received the baptism of the Holy Spirit believe they can now 'do great works for God,' without the need of total dependence and guidance of the Spirit. The lesson from the Bible is undeniable – we cannot achieve anything of any eternal value without Him!

"There is a great contradiction in saying the Lord's prayer, stating, 'Your will be done, Your Kingdom come,' whilst we spend our entire lives doing our own will and building our own kingdoms of sand," said a disciple of the Lord. "The difference between a person led by the Holy Spirit and a Christian who still relies on the abilities of the flesh can be very subtle. As we have not learnt to exercise the gift of discernment, it can be very difficult for the average believer to see the difference between two people building a ministry – one in the flesh, and the other by the Spirit.

"The flesh has dominated our lives for so long that many believers who have received the baptism of the Holy Spirit still rely on their own abilities to 'serve God.' The person who walks according to the flesh, is like a man with a torch walking in the darkness trying to see what he can do and where he can go in his own strength. He may succeed – yet none of it is in the Spirit. The person who walks in the Spirit is like a man who knows, 'Your Word is a lamp unto my feet,' and only steps forward when the Holy Spirit lights the step ahead (Psalm 119:105). Every step is a step of faith and the work is built by God Himself. However, there is such a mixture of the work of the Spirit and of the flesh in some ministries, that people are confused. The best thing for us all to do is to renounce all confidence in the flesh, and be led by the Holy Spirit and let Him do His work!"

We all need to spend time allowing the Holy Spirit to get hold of us and teach us the difference between being led by Him and trusting in self. This is why Rees Howells was drawn aside from others to be taught by the Holy Spirit. Rees Howells learnt God could provide, lead and direct him. These may seem basic ideas, but most of us do not know these basics. Many are still seeking to be led by good ideas and directed by others in our churches. The basics of walking with the Holy Spirit, knowing His voice, provision and guidance is still unknown by many Christians.

'There is no sadder sight on earth than that of a one-time Spirit-anointed preacher who has lost the unction from heaven but who still goes on preaching,' wrote Maynard James. 'The same phraseology is there, the same gestures and intonation. But the warmth and glow of the Holy Spirit are sadly missing. Some people in the audience may be deceived by play-acting. But the discerning saints realised in their hearts that the glory has departed.'[3]

After Rees Howells was possessed by the Holy Spirit, he saw the hypocrisy of an unsurrendered good Christian life. The Holy Spirit showed him that in the unsurrendered state he could spend much time asking God to meet many needs, and yet be totally unwilling for God to answer any prayer through him. The Holy Spirit revealed that the Lord is "wearied with our words" (Malachi 2:17). All this unreality and disobedience had to be put on one side.

When Rees Howells fulfilled the conditions of Romans 12:1, and laid down his life and will on the altar of the Lord, the Holy Spirit then applied His objectives in his life: intense cultivation leading to personal transformation and abounding fruitfulness by the Holy Spirit. But as 'the land' of his life was fallow ground, He had to till it acre by acre. In a practical sense, it meant allowing the Holy Spirit to lead him into situations where his old life died, and the new resurrected life of Christ was revealed in and through him.

In one crisis situation, Rees Howells was called to be prepared to help provide for orphaned children. "I am a Father of the fatherless," the Lord told him, "but I cannot be a Father to them in heaven, so I must be one through you." Rees Howells realised that his human nature could never love other people's children as his own. So he told the Lord, "I am willing for You to be a Father through me, but I cannot do it unless You love them through me, so that they are not like adopted, but begotten children; and to do that, You will have to change my nature." In this way, the nature of God, which is love, started to replace the selfish human nature and God was reaching out to the world, and meeting needs through Rees Howells.

In Rees Howells' experiences with the leading of the Holy Spirit, God's twofold purposes were evident. The first was the blessing of the needy (John 3:16), and the second, the transformation of his servant. "The Holy Ghost took me through grade after grade," Rees testified. "The process of changing one's nature (replacing self centred nature with the Divine nature) was very slow and bitter. It was a daily dying and showing forth the life of Christ, every selfish motive and selfish thought had to be dealt with by the Holy Spirit."

The Rev. Evan Hopkins said, "Shall we now look at the other question? How to have rivers of living water flowing from us. What is this blessing? Oh, it is a far greater blessing than the first, because it is more blessed to give than to receive. When the fullness begins to flow out, then you realise what you could not realise before – a deeper joy, a clearer vision, greater power and more courage.

"There is believing to see; there is believing to receive. Now we come to that other side, believing to give. I think many of us need to have that emphasised. 'He that believeth on Me, as the Scripture hath said, out of him shall flow rivers of living water.' It is very beautiful, when we look at the original. 'He that is putting faith in Me,' points to a continuous believing condition of the soul. It is not, 'he that believed on Me when he was converted,' nor, 'he that believed on Me when he entered into eternal life,' but it is, 'he that is believing on Me now.' The Spirit's out-flowing needs believing on our part, just as much as the Spirit's inflowing."[4]

"If our Lord has redeemed us at the price of His blood, we are purchased property and should be subject completely to His control," said Alan G. Morrell, speaking at Westminster Chapel London in 1946. "If He gave His life for us, He has a legitimate right to expect us to live for Him...the need of the present is overwhelming. The world is crying out in its utter and desperate need. The condition of the unheeding multitudes constitutes a permanent challenge to the spiritual man and woman. So Christ would say to your heart and mine, in view of the present, with all its need and opportunity, 'Lend Me thy body, for I need a body still to touch those for whom I died. I need hearts filled with My love, lips purged from every defilement and touched with holy fire, lives cleansed from all uncleanness, men and women who are willing to yield themselves unreservedly to Me.' Oh, I beseech you in view of the present, with all its urgent clamant need, to offer your body a living, loving sacrifice. Paul, living the consecrated life, could sum up his experience in those powerful words, 'I live, yet not I, but Christ liveth in me.' John the Baptist could say, 'He must increase, but I must decrease.' They had learnt the secret of unconditional surrender, the life of consecration and absolute fidelity and devotion to Christ."[5]

Dr. Chapman (1859-1918), a great evangelist, whilst in London had a brief meeting with General Booth, the founder of the Salvation Army. He said, "When I looked into his face and saw him brush his hair from his brow, heard him speak of the trials and conflicts and victories, I said, 'General Booth, tell me what has been the secret of your success all the way through.' He hesitated a moment, and then I saw the tears come into his eyes and steal down his cheeks; then he said, 'I will tell you the secret. God has had all there was of me. There have been men with greater brains than I, men with greater opportunities, but from the day I got the poor of London on my heart, and a vision of what Jesus Christ could do with the poor of London, I made up my mind that God should have all of William Booth there was, and if there is anything of power in the Salvation Army today, it is because God has had all the adorations of my heart, all my power of my will, and all the influence of my life.'

"Then he looked at me a moment, and I soon learned another secret of his power…he said, 'Pray with me.' I dropped on my knees with General Booth by my side and prayed a stammering, stuttering prayer; and then he talked with God about the outcasts of London, the poor of New York, the lost of China, the great world lying in wickedness, and then he opened his eyes as if he were looking into the face of Jesus, and with sobs he prayed God's blessing upon every mission worker, every evangelist, every minister, every Christian; and with his eyes still full of tears he bade me good-bye, and started away, past eighty years of age, to preach to the continent. And I learned from William Booth that the greatness of a man's power is the measure of his surrender. It is not a question of who you are or what you are, but whether God controls you, whether the Holy Spirit fills you with Himself!"[6]

*Questions to consider:* Are you a channel of the Holy Spirit? Does Christ live His life through you?

*Actions:* Ask the Holy Spirit if you have experienced this and invite Him to live His life through you.

## Chapter Thirty

## The Flesh is Useless

- Jesus said, "It is the Spirit who gives life; the flesh profits nothing. The words that I speak to you are spirit and they are life" (John 6:63).
- Jesus said, "If you love Me, keep My commandments. And I will pray the Father, and He will give you another Helper, that He may abide with you forever – the Spirit of Truth, whom the world cannot receive, because it neither sees Him nor knows Him; but you know Him, for He dwells with you and will be in you" (John 14:15-17).
- Jesus said, "But the Helper, the Holy Spirit, whom the Father will send in My name, He will teach you all things, and bring to your remembrance all things that I said to you" (John 14:26).
- Jesus said, "But when the Helper comes, whom I shall send to you from the Father, the Spirit of Truth who proceeds from the Father, He will testify of Me" (John 15:26).
- Jesus said, "However, when He, the Spirit of Truth has come, He will guide you into all truth; for He will not speak on His own authority, but whatever He hears He will speak, and He will tell you things to come. He will glorify Me, for He will take of what is Mine and declare it to you. All things that the Father has are Mine. Therefore, I said that He will take of Mine and declare it to you" (John 16:13-15).
- Jesus said, "But when they deliver you up, do not worry about how or what you should speak. For it will be given to you in that hour what you should speak; for it is not you who speak, but the Spirit of your Father who speaks in you" (Matthew 10:19-20).
- Jesus said, "Now when they bring you to the synagogues and magistrates and authorities, do not worry about how or what you should answer or what you should say. For the Holy Spirit will teach you in that very hour what you ought to say" (Luke 12:11-12).
- Jesus said, "For it is not you who speak, but the Holy Spirit" (Mark 13:11).
- 'Walk in the Spirit and you shall not fulfil the lust of the flesh. For the flesh lusts against the Spirit and the Spirit against the flesh; and these are contrary to one another, so that you do not do the things that you wish' (Galatians 5:16-17).

# Chapter Thirty-One

## The Pruning of the Master

When we invite the Holy Spirit into our lives, we may believe that He will instantly make everything perfect without the need for us to change, but this is never the case. Jesus taught that if we abide in Him, the Father will come as the Vinedresser and cut off any branch in our lives that does not bear fruit. Instead of all our energy being wasted on dead works, the Lord will come into our lives and take away that which will not bear fruit. Jesus said, "I am the true Vine, and My Father is the Vinedresser. Every branch in Me that does not bear fruit He takes away; and every branch that bears fruit He prunes, that it may bear more fruit" (John 15:1-3).

"The Holy Spirit wants to release us from the power of self – our own self will and the hold the world has on us," said a disciple of the Lord. "The Bible tells us God has a specific, detailed plan and purpose for every life (Ephesians 2:10). Nevertheless we are also told that we must 'walk in' that plan. This reveals we can walk away from that plan or resist that plan and ignore it. Therefore, to remove our natural resistance to obeying God, He will come as the Great Vinedresser and will prune our lives. He will cut out dead activities, dead friendships and dead past times. This is not a deep spiritual exercise devoid of real life, but it is a very realistic transformation of one's life. He comes and cuts off all the dead branches in our lives. He prunes, removes, cuts and burns. Then, He comes and fills areas once controlled by the flesh, with His Spirit. But God does not do any of this without our agreement – we have to give Him the role as our Vinedresser and we must allow Him to get pruning in our lives. We are reminded: 'If we live in the Spirit, let us also walk in the Spirit' (Galatians 5:24–25). This means we must not only receive the Spirit, but we must walk into His path and plan, as the Vinedresser does His work."

C.S. Lewis wrote of this pruning: 'Christ says, "Give me *all*. I don't want so much of your time, and so much of your money and so much of your work: I want *you*. I have not come to torment your natural self, but to kill it. No half measures are any good. I don't want to cut off a branch here and a branch there, I want to have the whole tree down. I don't want to drill the tooth, or crown it, or stop it, but to have it out. Hand over the whole natural self, all the desires which you think innocent as well as the ones you think wicked – the whole outfit. I will give you a new self instead. In fact, I will give you

Myself: My own will shall become yours"...We are all trying to let our mind and heart go their own way – centred on money or pleasure or ambition – and hoping, in spite of this, to behave honestly and chastely and humbly. And that is exactly what Christ warned us you could not do. As He said, a thistle cannot produce figs (Matthew 7:16-20). If I am a field that contains nothing but grass seed, I cannot produce wheat. Cutting the grass may keep it short: but I shall still produce grass and no wheat. If I want to produce wheat, the change must go deeper than the surface. I must be ploughed up and re-sown'[1] (Jeremiah 4:3, Hosea 10:12).

To lead us to be fruit bearing as God desires, the Holy Spirit will guide us into a time of intense pruning in our lives. He will take away all crutches that we have relied upon, and will cut them out of our lives. We have many branches that draw off 'the sap' in our lives; there are things that take up our time, money, effort and emotions, yet produce no fruit for the Kingdom. In a practical sense the Holy Spirit may cut off friendships, useless church meetings, ritualised prayer, good works and anything else in our lives that takes our strength, and time, yet produces no lasting fruit.

To the natural mind the ways of God can seem very unreasonable. We cannot always understand what God is doing and why. It is a process of faith, but in the fullness of time we may look back and say, "Now, I know why!" The process of allowing God to prune our lives and cut off branches may feel like 'an attack' on our way of life. Without God's wisdom it may seem like a very dark experience, yet as time goes by we will learn that He takes away all the 'branches' in our lives that will never produce fruit, in order that our strength, energy, money, time, effort, and prayers can be focused exclusively on producing the spiritual fruit which He calls forth and desires.

"Once you surrender to the Holy Spirit He is always trying to teach you something," said a disciple of the Lord. "Once I was visiting relatives who had important positions in a church and the Holy Spirit said to me, 'I never want you to return here again. They will belittle your faith.' That direction is very hard for most believers to accept, but God spoke to Jeremiah, Ezekiel, Isaiah, Hosea and to the disciples, giving them costly directions (Luke 9:60). The Spirit is very sensitive and is grieved by those who call Jesus Lord, yet are unwilling to obey Him (John 14:15). Those who reject the will of the Spirit are the spiritually dead and will be a hinderance to those who go on with the Lord" (Matthew 8:22, 1 Corinthians 15:33).

This experience and many others like it are a part of the Lord's strategy to get us to focus all our strength on the life and work He has for us. He is pruning, cutting and it will hurt, but it will make us more fruitful. The Holy Spirit will lead disciples of the Lord to end friendships and withdraw from the 'Christian' people who are not following the Lord with their whole heart.

"In 1 Corinthians 5:11, Paul explains the need to withdraw from people who claim to follow God, who are not living the life," said a disciple of the Lord. "I read this passage many times, but the Holy Spirit made it real to me when He made it specific in my life and told me to end friendships. There are many passages in the Bible that deal with this subject, but it is the Holy Spirit who made this Scripture come alive to me (Proverbs 12:26, 13:30). Now decades on, my old friends are still in the spiritual slumber of sin and rebellion, and God has led me on further and deeper into Him."

The Father as the Vinedresser has the right to come into our lives and cut out any hobby, interest or anything that is a 'dead branch' sucking the life out of us. Giving up the old life is a part of living the crucified life. Bible School Principal John D. Drysdale wrote in 1946: 'The sad feature about much of our evangelical Christianity is that so many want all the benefits of His cross without being willing to take up their cross and follow Christ; and one wonders if it is possible to have one without the other."[2]

When we welcome the Holy Spirit into our lives in all His fullness, we do not receive trouble-free lives, but instead He exercises the Lordship of Christ in and through us. "The fullness of the Spirit does not dispense with the trial and the exercise of faith," said the Rev. Evan Hopkins. "Faith is not now replaced by feeling. The soul that is filled with the Holy Ghost does not feel full; there is no self-sufficiency," he preached. "Right along throughout the whole life there will be the testing, there will be the trial of faith, and there will be the need of the perpetual exercise of faith just as at present, only on another level. Many of us are thinking, 'If I get the fullness of the Spirit, I shall have plenty of power, plenty of wisdom, plenty of knowledge, and I shall have a very easy time.' Well, the full life is the easy life. 'My yoke is easy,' said Christ. But it cannot be apart from the exercise of faith.

"Ease comes by believing, and by having your own emptiness met by His fullness...You have an impression, too, that if you only get this full life, you will not need to be so vigilant and prayerful, or to be looking up for power. Well, look at Acts 4. Here were men, after Pentecost, who had been filled with the Holy Ghost; but how childlike and dependent they are, how conscious of their own nothingness and weakness! You see how weak, how conscious of their nothingness, how utterly dependent they were upon the Lord, after Pentecost; how they had to pray, how they had to exercise faith, how they realised the power of the Name of Christ, and how conscious they were that apart from God, they must fail. And this will be your experience and mine, right on to the end. But, oh, to know that God is here and in us, that we have the fullness of God! You see the paradox – 'As having nothing, and yet possessing all things' (2 Corinthians 6:10). God's strength being made perfect in our weakness."[3]

To prepare us for a deeper life of pruning, the Spirit will lead us like Jesus into the wilderness. 'Then Jesus was led up by the Spirit into the wilderness to be tempted by the devil' (Matthew 4:1). The spiritual desert will be a time of testing, trials and struggle. We may witness no miracles and we may be forsaken by all. We may hunger and thirst, and fight endless battles with little sight of victory. The thought of giving up on this life with the Spirit will be a temptation, but the desire to go on will be written too deep within us.

The wilderness is not a physical place for us, like it was for Jesus, but we can be in a wilderness anywhere. Many of the servants of God in the Bible had their own wilderness experiences. The obvious example will be Moses, who spent forty years being broken and made contrite in heart for his future in God's will. Jesus spent forty days, where the human flesh was brought into total submission to the will of the Father, as the devil threw every power of hell against Him. He came out of the experience 'in the power of the Spirit' (Luke 4:14), and Jesus Christ's miraculous ministry began! One preacher explained how the wilderness experience changed the apostles, with the subsequent baptism of the Spirit: "Before Pentecost, the apostles wanted everything and had nothing; after Pentecost they wanted nothing and had everything."

This deeper place with God will be a great challenge to many and we may find ourselves as strangers to many, even within the Church (Exodus 33:7). 'For all seek their own, not the things which are of Christ Jesus' (Philippians 2:21).

Through these experiences we learn that the Holy Spirit is often an outcast and a stranger in the very place where He is supposed to be honoured. Michael Harper wrote: 'The Church tends to honour its revolutionary sons and daughters when they are safely buried. It closes the doors of its churches to its prophets and then builds monuments to them and fills its hymn books with their compositions, as it did to the Wesleys. It prefers dead saints to living revolutionaries. Human nature has not changed much since Christ charged the religious leaders of His day with doing the same thing'[4] (Matthew 23:29-34).

*Questions to consider:* Are you allowing the Lord to prune and cut out things in your life? Have you welcomed the fire of God?

*Actions:* Allow God to be your Vinedresser. Listen to Him and accept His pruning.

# Chapter Thirty-Two

## The True Vine

- Jesus said, "I am the true Vine and My Father is the Vinedresser. Every branch in Me that does not bear fruit He takes away; and every branch that bears fruit He prunes, that it may bear more fruit...Abide in Me, and I in you. As the branch cannot bear fruit of itself, unless it abides in the Vine, neither can you, unless you abide in Me. I am the Vine, you are the branches. He who abides in Me, and I in him, bears much fruit; for without Me you can do nothing. If anyone does not abide in Me, he is cast out as a branch and is withered; and they gather them and throw them into the fire, and they are burned" (John 15:1-6).
- Jesus said, "No longer do I call you servants, for a servant does not know what his master is doing; but I have called you friends, for all things that I heard from My Father I have made known to you. You did not choose Me, but I chose you and appointed you that you should go and bear fruit, and that your fruit should remain, that whatever you ask the Father in My name He may give you. These things I command you, that you love one another" (John 15:15-17).
- Jesus said, "Remember the Word that I said to you, 'A servant is not greater than his master.' If they persecuted Me, they will also persecute you. If they kept My Word, they will keep yours also. But all these things they will do to you for My name's sake, because they do not know Him who sent Me" (John 15:20-21).
- Jesus said, "But when the Helper comes, whom I shall send to you from the Father, the Spirit of Truth who proceeds from the Father, He will testify of Me. And you also will bear witness, because you have been with Me from the beginning" (John 15:26-27).
- 'If we love one another, God abides in us, and His love has been perfected in us. By this we know that we abide in Him, and He in us, because He has given us of His Spirit. And we have seen and testify that the Father has sent the Son as Saviour of the world. Whoever confesses that Jesus is the Son of God, God abides in him, and he in God. And we have known and believed the love that God has for us. God is love, and he who abides in love abides in God, and God in him' (1 John 4:12-16).

# Chapter Thirty-Three

## Being One with Him

As we continue to walk with the Lord and unconditionally obey Him, we will discover that the pruning process and life of abiding can lead us to being separated to the Lord, in a place of abiding which few understand. In that secret place, we discover that the greater the fire of God in our lives, the more He burns up the dross, and we lose our lives in Him. Through this process, we discover what Paul meant when he wrote: 'I have been crucified with Christ; it is no longer I who live, but Christ lives in me' (Galatians 2:20). This was not a vague declaration of faith, but the reality of his life. The old Paul, remembered as Saul of Tarsus died many years before, and now Christ was living His life through him (Acts 7:58, 9:11). Paul's old life – his thoughts, dreams, ideas and even theology were finished; that man died with Christ.

Someone once asked George Müller to explain the secret to his successful Christian ministry. He said, "There was a day that I died. There was a day when I died, utterly died – died to George Müller, his opinions, preferences, tastes and will; died to the world, its approval or censure; died to the approval or blame even of my brethren and friends – and since then I have only to show myself approved to God."

'If God has called you to be truly like Jesus in all your spirit, He will draw you into a life of crucifixion and humility," wrote the evangelist G.D. Watson (1845-1924), as he explained what it means to have died to this world, to live a crucified life, so Christ lives through us. 'He will put on you such demands of obedience that you will not be allowed to follow other Christians. In many ways, He seems to let other good people do things which He will not let you do. Others who seem to be very religious and useful may push themselves, pull wires, and scheme to carry out their plans, but you cannot. If you attempt it, you will meet with such failure and rebuke from the Lord as to make you sorely penitent. Others can brag about themselves, their work, their successes, their writings, but the Holy Spirit will not allow you to do any such thing. If you begin to do so, He will lead you into some deep mortification that will make you despise yourself and all your good works. Others will be allowed to succeed in making great sums of money, or having a legacy left to them, or in having luxuries, but God may supply you only on a day-to-day basis, because He wants you to have something far better than gold, a helpless dependence on Him and His unseen treasury.

'The Lord may let others be honoured and put forward while keeping you hidden in obscurity because He wants to produce some choice fragrant fruit for His coming glory, which can only be produced in the shade. God may let others be great, but keep you small. He will let others do a work for Him and get the credit, but He will make you work and toil on without knowing how much you are doing. Then, to make your work still more precious, He will let others get the credit for the work which you have done to teach you the message of the cross, humility, and something of the value of being cloaked with His nature. The Holy Spirit will put a strict watch on you, and with a jealous love rebuke you for careless words and feelings, or for wasting your time which other Christians never seem distressed over. So make up your mind that God is an infinite Sovereign and has a right to do as He pleases with His own, and that He may not explain to you a thousand things which may puzzle your reason in His dealings with you.

'God will take you at your word; if you absolutely sell yourself to be His slave, He will wrap you up in a jealous love and let other people say and do many things that you cannot. Settle it forever; you are to deal directly with the Holy Spirit, He is to have the privilege of tying your tongue or chaining your hand or closing your eyes in ways which others are not dealt with. However, know this great secret of the Kingdom – when you are so completely possessed with the Living God that you are, in your secret heart, pleased and delighted over this peculiar, personal, private, jealous guardianship and management of the Holy Spirit over your life, you will have found the vestibule of heaven, the high calling of God.'

Many of the greatest servants of God have never told their stories. When an individual has truly seen the cross and died with his or her Lord, the concept of achieving wealth or fame in Christian circles become meaningless. These people enter into a realm that defies all convention; they seek an audience with One – the Lord Himself. 'You shall give them no possession in Israel, for I am their possession' (Ezekiel 44:28). "We are not seeking popularity are we?" asked Samuel Rees Howells at his Bible College. "It was a cross that was given to our Lord. The popularity of the religious, of the evangelical world – what does that mean? To a true man of God, a man that has been to the cross and is broken at the cross – what does it mean?"[1] (Galatians 2:20).

*Questions to consider:* Are you becoming one with the Lord and His will? Do you live His life?

*Actions:* Seek the Lord for a deeper oneness with Him and throw any hinderance aside.

# Chapter Thirty-Four

## Jesus, One with the Spirit

- 'Now the birth of Jesus Christ was as follows: After His mother Mary was betrothed to Joseph, before they came together, she was found with child of the Holy Spirit' (Matthew 1:18).
- 'The Holy Spirit descended in bodily form like a dove upon Him and a Voice came from heaven which said, "You are My beloved Son; in You I am well pleased" ' (Luke 3:22).
- 'Immediately the Spirit drove Him into the wilderness. And He was there in the wilderness forty days, tempted by Satan, and was with the wild beasts; and the angels ministered to Him' (Mark 1:12-13).
- Jesus said, "The Spirit of the Lord is upon Me, because He has anointed Me to preach the gospel to the poor. He has sent Me to heal the broken-hearted, to proclaim liberty to the captives and recovery of sight to the blind, to set at liberty those who are oppressed; to proclaim the acceptable year of the Lord" (Luke 4:18-19).
- 'John bore witness, saying, "I saw the Spirit descending from heaven like a dove, and He remained upon Him. I did not know Him, but He who sent me to baptise with water said to me, 'Upon whom you see the Spirit descending, and remaining on Him, this is He who baptises with the Holy Spirit.' And I have seen and testified that this is the Son of God" ' (John 1:32-24).
- 'Who through the Spirit of holiness was appointed the Son of God in power by His resurrection from the dead: Jesus Christ our Lord' (Romans 1:4).
- 'Therefore I want you to know that no one who is speaking by the Spirit of God says, "Jesus be cursed," and no one can say, "Jesus is Lord," except by the Holy Spirit' (1 Corinthians 12:3).
- 'He appeared in the flesh, was vindicated by the Spirit, was seen by angels, was preached among the nations, was believed on in the world, was taken up in glory' (1 Timothy 3:16).
- 'Hold fast the pattern of sound words which you have heard from me, in faith and love which are in Christ Jesus. That good thing which was committed to you, keep by the Holy Spirit who dwells in us' (2 Timothy 1:13-14).
- 'This is He who came by water and blood – Jesus Christ; not only by water, but by water and blood. And it is the Spirit who bears witness, because the Spirit is Truth' (1 John 5:6).

# Chapter Thirty-Five

## The Holy Spirit as Intercessor

When human prayer comes to an end, real praying begins. When our lists of wants are surrendered at the cross, Holy Spirit praying can commence. The Holy Spirit needs a body through whom He can intercede, but He will not share His glory with another. Thus, after we have witnessed the blessing of His miraculous ways, He will guide us into circumstances leading to the death of our reputations. The purpose of these great pruning experiences is to prepare us for the greater unseen working of the Holy Spirit, perhaps through intercession, or another hidden work. This is the route that all the prophets and apostles walked. John the Baptist was led into the solitude of the wilderness of God and was transformed into the last prophet of the old dispensation, and was given revelations which led to the opening of the ministry of Jesus (Mark 1:1-8, Luke 16:16).

"Most Christians are confused about the difference between prayer and intercession," said a disciple of the Lord. "Yet in the teaching of Christ in John 15, in the testimony of the apostles and in the lives of the prophets it is clear! When we pray, the emphasis is on 'we or I,' going to prayer! It is our prayer, or my prayer and desire. When we pray, we hope God will answer it, and we hope it is according to His will. However, in intercession, it is the Holy Spirit who prays and intercedes. The intercessor only prays what the Holy Spirit asks him or her to plead. Prayer often begins with us, but intercession always begins with the Holy Spirit. It is He who tells the intercessor to pray this or that. It is He, the Holy Spirit who gives the terms and conditions of the intercession.

"This is what abiding is – often the Holy Spirit asks the intercessor to meet some practical obligation to prove the depth of the intercession. He may ask the intercessor to fast, to give, to change one's attitude to become more Christ like etc. Then, as the intercessor follows the will of the Holy Spirit, He prays through the believer with groans that cannot be uttered (Romans 8:26). When the Holy Spirit lays an intercession on a believer, that person is committed to the intercession – to pray it daily, hourly and in every minute until it is answered. I don't mean having a prayer time every minute, but living out the intercession in one's life – it is always on one's heart (1 Thessalonians 5:17). It is His intercession and burden being prayed through His vessel.

"In a prayer meeting we finish 'our' praying and go away and forget, but the intercessor is never free of the intercession until the

Holy Spirit releases him or her. It is on him or her all day everyday. They can be doing a number of things, but the thought, burden and intercession is always present. Intercession is so very different from believers praying what they think they want or need. It's another world altogether and only the Holy Spirit – the Teacher Himself can reveal it to you and in you."

Rees Howells was pondering the question of the intercession of the Holy Spirit, whom 'makes intercession for us with groanings which cannot be uttered' (Romans 8:26), when he read that prayer moves forward the plan of God on earth. Commenting on Matthew 9:38, "Pray the Lord of the harvest to send forth labourers into His harvest," Andrew Murray indicated that the number of missionaries seeking to win the lost, depends entirely on the extent to which Christians obey that command and prays out the labourers. Suddenly Rees Howells understood that the Lord was calling him to do this, and that nothing, even though prophesied beforehand in Scripture, can come to pass unless God finds empty channels who will intercede for His purposes to unfold. Prophecies therefore must be believed into manifestation, as well as foretold (Daniel 9:2-4).

Rees Howells came to understand that it is not the Christian who is the intercessor, but the Holy Spirit within him who was interceding. This Person, the only real Intercessor on earth, has no hearts upon which He can lay His burdens, and no bodies through which He can suffer and work, except the hearts and bodies of those who choose to be His dwelling place (Isaiah 59:16). Through these surrendered vessels the Holy Spirit undertakes His intercessory work on earth (Ezekiel 22:30). Missionary to Japan, Paget Wilkes wrote: 'Only the man of prayer will be full of power. Only the man full of the Holy Ghost will be a man of prayer.'[1]

In Rees Howells' experience, the needs of the world were so vast, that it is was necessary for him to hear very clearly the direct leading of the Spirit. To do this, he had to be impartial in any crisis because only the impartial can find God's will. The vital question in every crisis he saw was to find the exact will of God.

The prophets of the Bible were often great intercessors and the Holy Spirit led them to make great sacrifices and live strange lives, compared to the average life. Consequently, the life of intercession will never be a simple one and will be misunderstood. In these cases we must accept the wisdom of Max Warren, who wrote in 1954: 'Final judgments about the work of the Spirit are best left to the Spirit who is, after all, the Spirit of judgment and can be trusted to do His own work.'[2]

Much praying in churches can be summarised as the proclamation of a number of wish lists of selfish desires, to pacify the flesh (James 4:3). Holy Spirit led intercession is the opposite – it is God's perfect revealed will being prayed into being by selfless intercessors saying, "Your Kingdom come, Your will be done, on earth as it is in heaven" (Matthew 6:10).

There is no title of intercessor in the Ephesians 4 list of positions of leaders, because the Holy Spirit Himself is the Intercessor on earth; thus, the call to intercession can come upon anyone within or outside of the five-fold ministry positions. A clear example of this is found in the chronicles of ministry of the apostles; they all gave themselves to prayer. "We will give ourselves continually to prayer and to the ministry of the Word" (Acts 6:4).

The Spirit is the Intercessor on earth, because human strength and will can never sustain the burden of an enduring intercession. The excitement and enthusiasm of the flesh upon commencement of any intercession can quickly melt away when the real battle begins. Intercession, when viewed with hindsight may appear very romantic, yet battles are often won as the enemy is evicted one field at a time.

Only the Spirit can lead us into intercession, but some Christians may find their prayer lives blending into intercession, when they are led to pray in tongues. When the Holy Spirit prays through us using this heavenly language, we will be praying perfect prayers, and our spirits are edified when we pray in tongues: 'Anyone who speaks in a tongue edifies themselves' (1 Corinthians 14:4). Praying in tongues is the ability to pray perfect prayers, with the benefit of spiritual edification from God and it may lead into an intercession.

Praying in tongues is not intercession in and of itself; but if the Spirit is leading us into intercession, He may use this form of prayer to guide us into an intercession with groans that cannot be uttered. When we pray in tongues our minds do not understand and may wander, so Paul writes: 'So what shall I do? I will pray with my spirit, but I will also pray with my understanding; I will sing with my spirit, but I will also sing with my understanding' (1 Corinthians 14:15).

Intercession cannot be understood with the carnal mind and our sinful nature can hinder our knowledge of its true power. This is why the Scriptures explain that the Spirit will help us: 'In the same way, the Spirit helps us in our weakness. We do not know what we ought to pray for, but the Spirit Himself intercedes for us through wordless groans' (Romans 8:26). For 'when the enemy comes in like a flood, the Spirit of the Lord will raise up a standard against him' (Isaiah 59:19).

*Questions to consider:* Will you be willing to be a vessel through whom the Holy Spirit can intercede? Do you realise that the Holy Spirit is the Intercessor on earth and Christ intercedes in heaven?

*Actions:* Prepare your heart and open your spirit to allow the Holy Spirit to place an intercession upon you, in His perfect timing.

# Chapter Thirty-Six

## The Intercession of the Spirit of God

### The Holy Spirit Leads in Prayer and Intercession
- 'The Spirit helps us in our weakness. We do not know what we ought to pray for, but the Spirit Himself intercedes for us through wordless groans. And He who searches our hearts knows the mind of the Spirit, because the Spirit intercedes for God's people in accordance with the will of God' (Romans 8:26-27).
- 'Take the helmet of salvation and the sword of the Spirit, which is the Word of God; praying always with all prayer and supplication in the Spirit, being watchful to this end with all perseverance and supplication for all the saints' (Ephesians 6:17-18).
- 'Building yourselves up in your most holy faith and praying in the Holy Spirit' (Jude 20).
- 'On the Lord's Day I was in the Spirit and I heard behind me a loud voice like a trumpet' (Revelation 1:10).
- 'At once I was in the Spirit and there before me was a throne in heaven with someone sitting on it' (Revelation 4:2).

### The Spirit of Intercession
- 'The Spirit of God' (Genesis 1:2, Exodus 31:3).
- 'The Spirit of your Father' (Matthew 10:20).
- 'The Spirit' (Numbers 27:18).
- 'The Spirit of the Lord' (Judges 3:10).
- 'Your Spirit' (Nehemiah 9:30).
- 'The Spirit of the Lord... Wisdom... Understanding... Counsel... Might... Knowledge... and the Fear of the Lord' (Isaiah 11:2).
- 'The Spirit of the Holy God' (Daniel 5:11).
- 'The Spirit of Grace' (Zechariah 12:10).
- 'The Spirit of Holiness' (Romans 1:4).
- 'The Spirit of Adoption' (Romans 8:15).
- 'The Spirit of our God' (1 Corinthians 6:11).
- 'The Spirit of the Living God' (2 Corinthians 3:3).
- 'The Spirit of the Lord' (2 Corinthians 3:18).
- 'The Holy Spirit of Promise' (Ephesians 1:13).
- 'The Spirit of Jesus Christ' (Philippians 1:19).
- 'The Holy Spirit' (Titus 3:5).
- 'The Eternal Spirit' (Hebrews 9:14).

# Chapter Thirty-Seven

## Abiding in the Vine

As time goes on in our walk with the Lord, we will learn not only the voice of the Holy Spirit, but His ways. He may begin to speak to us without words, because our experiences lead us to know His ways, as well as His voice. God is all knowing and thus, He already knows our thoughts, and can share His desires with us without the need of speech (Galatians 4:6). In this case, we just 'know' what needs to be done. In this walk with God, He will lead us to lay deep foundations in Christ. Due to this we will no longer need the 'big' miracles to encourage us to go on with Him. The spectacular aspects of our walk with God in the past may have strengthened us to press through testing times, but as we progress we learn that He has come to abide in us and is always with us, as we are in Him.

Jesus said, "Abide in Me and I in you. As the branch cannot bear fruit of itself, unless it abides in the vine, neither can you, unless you abide in Me. I am the Vine, you are the branches. He who abides in Me, and I in him, bears much fruit; for without Me you can do nothing" (John 15:4-5). He awaits our response (Revelation 3:20).

"The Spirit thinks the thoughts of God," said a disciple of the Lord. "The Bible states: 'In the same way no one knows the thoughts of God except the Spirit of God...' (1 Corinthians 2:10). If we are walking in the Spirit, some of those thoughts will spill over into our consciousness. Sometimes God shares His thoughts with us, just because He wants to share with His friends (John 15:15); this is one of the benefits of abiding in Him, as we get to see the world, the Church and reality from His perspective."

Rees Howells witnessed many healings, conversions, impossible breakthroughs, revivals and Divine provision. In every case Rees Howells was simply following the Lord's direction, and abiding in His will and revelation. What does abiding mean? Rees Howells found that the necessity for abiding in the Lord is essential for any victory in Christ. He learnt that all the life in the Church is in the Vine. As the branch remains united to it by abiding in it, that life of the Vine produces the fruit through the branch. In other words, the power is in Christ. As we are united to Him by abiding in Him, His power operates through us and accomplishes what needs to be done.

For Rees Howells and for us, abiding will remain being constantly aware of the Presence of Christ in all that we do. He is with us at all times and because we want Him to dwell and abide with us, we live holy lives. The Rev. Evan Hopkins said, "Then we are prepared for intimate and uninterrupted fellowship with God. And now naturally follows the sense of Divine ownership and possession we feel that we are God's, and that there is no reserved territory in our being. Then we come into the true life of rest and peace, when darkness flees away and His light floods us. And then, and then only, are we fit for that wider influence and authoritative witness which comes with the filling of the Holy Spirit."[1]

"One of the great lessons from the life of Rees Howells and of his son, Samuel Rees Howells, is we must only pray the prayers given to us by the Holy Spirit," said a disciple of the Lord. "Much time in the Church is wasted in saying prayers which we have no confidence shall be answered. John testified: 'Now this is the confidence that we have in Him, that if we ask anything according to His will, He hears us' (1 John 5:14). How can we know His will? The answer is simple – we must walk closely with the Holy Spirit and allow Him to reveal the Lord's will to us. The Holy Spirit knows the thoughts of God the Father, therefore we must draw close to the Spirit in abiding faith in the Lord Jesus Christ (1 Corinthians 2:10). This means we must live in the spotlight of the Holy Spirit. What is this spotlight? It is the Divine spotlight of abiding in His direct and stated will. When we live in that spotlight we are not free to step outside of the Divine guidance shining down from heaven, on the exact spot and position our lives should be in. The flesh is full of great ideas of how to serve God, but the Bible states the flesh should be crucified and the Spirit should be leading us!

"People sometimes think it is easy to walk this close with God; it is, and it is not. The simplicity of this walk is found in obeying God. The complexity is being sure of His exact will and purposes. Sometimes He speaks and we can misinterpret what He says, or read the wrong side of the coin of His will. If I ever walk outside of His Divine spotlight, I feel the darkness around and realise my mistake, and have to walk back into the light. To me, this is what it means in part to abide in God; to do exactly what He says and stay in the spotlight of His will, and in the specific acts of abiding if in an intercession. As the Scripture states: 'If we walk in the light as He is in the light, we have fellowship with one another...' " (1 John 1:7).

Rees Howells also learnt the importance of specific acts of abiding in the life of intercession. If he was to get God's prayer answered, which the Holy Spirit laid upon him, he must not only abide in the Lord in holiness, but become one with the specific acts of abiding laid on him by the Holy Spirit. Sometimes Rees Howells was asked to fast, give, sacrifice, or take on another's responsibility etc., until the prayer he was abiding in was answered. The Spirit of God gave Rees John 15:7 –"If you abide in Me and My words abide in you, you will ask what you desire, and it shall be done for you." This

Scripture makes it plain that the promise is unlimited, but its fulfilment depends on the abiding. With this in mind, Rees Howells constantly spoke of guarding his 'place of abiding.'

The Holy Spirit showed Rees Howells that if he wanted answers to prayer, he must only pray the prayers that were given to him by the Holy Spirit (1 John 5:14). In that way, Rees Howells would never waste time pleading prayers that were not according to the big picture of God's will (Acts 16:7, James 4:3). Thus, all selfish prayers would drop to the ground and die. In this way the Lord taught Rees that the needy in the world would always get the fruit of his abiding. The Holy Spirit showed him, "I have grafted you into the Vine and all the sap can flow through you. You are a branch in the Saviour. The branch gets nothing, for it is the needy that get the fruit."

The Scriptural key to abiding is: 'He who says he abides in Him ought himself also to walk just as He walked' (1 John 2:6). In other words, it meant that Rees Howells must be willing for the Holy Spirit to live through him the life the Saviour would have lived, if He had been in his place. Any command the Holy Spirit gave him, he must fulfil, because his abiding meant the keeping of all the Lord's commandments: "If you keep My commandments, you will abide in My love, just as I have kept My Father's commandments and abide in His love" (John 15:10).

As Rees Howells moved on from small answers to prayer, to larger world-shaking intercessions he discovered there are degrees and stages in abiding. The deeper the oneness with God, the more the power of the risen life of Christ can operate through the channel and positions of spiritual authority can be gained (Philippians 3:10). This was what all the prophets of the Old Testament experienced and it is evident in the lives of the apostles.

During many important intercessions given to Rees Howells by the Holy Spirit he said, "The Lord kept me daily and hourly abiding, to fulfil the condition for claiming an answer to my prayers." When he was leading others to pray for the protection of Britain during WWII, Rees said, "Can you say you are safe in the air raids? Has God told you? You may try to use the Word of God without having His power behind it." He was learning that we must abide in the Lord for His purposes in our lives, but we must also have specific places of abiding in the intercessions God gives to us and we must be committed to that abiding until the prayer has been answered.

*Questions to consider:* Are you abiding in the Lord? Have you been given a place of abiding?

*Actions:* Ask the Lord to show you how to abide in the spotlight of His will. Seek Him for guidance.

# Chapter Thirty-Eight

## Searching All Things

### The Holy Spirit Searches All Things

- 'These are the things God has revealed to us by His Spirit. The Spirit searches all things, even the deep things of God. For who knows a person's thoughts except their own spirit within them? In the same way no one knows the thoughts of God except the Spirit of God. What we have received is not the spirit of the world, but the Spirit who is from God' (1 Corinthians 2:10-11).
- 'The person without the Spirit does not accept the things that come from the Spirit of God but considers them foolishness, and cannot understand them because they are discerned only through the Spirit' (1 Corinthians 2:14).
- 'Do not believe every spirit, but test the spirits to see whether they are from God, because many false prophets have gone out into the world. This is how you can recognise the Spirit of God: Every spirit that acknowledges that Jesus Christ has come in the flesh is from God, but every spirit that does not acknowledge Jesus is not from God. This is the spirit of the antichrist, which you have heard is coming and even now is already in the world' (1 John 4:1-3).
- 'Dear friends, remember what the apostles of our Lord Jesus Christ foretold. They said to you, "In the last times there will be scoffers who will follow their own ungodly desires." These are the people who divide you, who follow mere natural instincts and do not have the Spirit' (Jude 17-19).

### Serving in Newness of the Spirit

- 'But now, by dying to what once bound us, we have been released from the law so that we serve in the new way of the Spirit, and not in the old way of the written code' (Romans 7:6).
- 'But the fruit of the Spirit is love, joy, peace, longsuffering, kindness, goodness, faithfulness, gentleness, self-control. Against such there is no law' (Galatians 5:22-23).
- 'Do not be deceived, God is not mocked; for whatever a man sows, that he will also reap. For he who sows to his flesh will of the flesh reap corruption, but he who sows to the Spirit will of the Spirit reap everlasting life' (Galatians 6:7-8).
- 'God chose you as firstfruits to be saved through the sanctifying work of the Spirit and through belief' (2 Thessalonians 2:13).

# Chapter Thirty-Nine

## Christ the Victor

In Western culture, we have been taught that blessings, curses, demons, and principalities and powers etc., are nonsense and were primitive beliefs systems displaying the ignorance of our forefathers. However, if we are to let the Holy Spirit be our Teacher and Guide, we must allow Him to open our eyes to our ignorance, pride and foolishness in all areas. God's Word is truth and our ever-changing culture is the lie. We are spiritual people, living in a spiritual world, which presently chooses to ignore Divine truths and principles.

Consequently, the first step in having our eyes open to the truth is to lay our pride and ignorance on the altar, and invite the Spirit of Truth to lead us into all truth. The Spirit will always lead us to the Bible, as the source of all truth and in the teaching of the Scriptures our ignorance will give way to God's revelation of reality.

In the Bible we learn that all people on earth are living in a titanic spiritual battle between God and Satan. At stake are the souls of every human, and the ultimate will and plan of God for the world. Yet, we are on the victory side because the resurrection of Jesus Christ has set the course for the ultimate defeat of Satan. Now, the resurrected Christ is Lord of all – souls can be saved, lands can be redeemed, principalities and powers can be routed by Holy Spirit intercession, every curse can be broken and every demon can be cast out and off people in Jesus' name (Matthew 28:18, Luke 9:1).

The Bible points us to the real battle we are in: 'For we do not wrestle against flesh and blood, but against principalities, against powers, against the rulers of this dark age, against spiritual hosts of wickedness in the heavenly places' (Ephesians 6:12). Therefore our warfare is spiritual and Christians who are walking with God have no need to fear the enemy because Jesus has defeated him.

'For this purpose the Son of God was manifested that He might destroy the works of the devil' (1 John 3:8). We have been given spiritual armour to wear (Ephesians 6:10-18). We have the Word of God to plead (Isaiah 55:11, Hebrews 4:12), and at the powerful name of Jesus demons flee (Matthew 28:18-20, Acts 4:10). We can plead the precious blood of Jesus (Ephesians 1:7, 2:13), as we stand in the authority of Jesus Christ (Romans 8:17, Galatians 4:7).

When the Holy Spirit opens our eyes to these truths He will also show us that He is the only Person who can give us the keys to victory in Christ. We can claim Scripture, shout, scream, and try to bind and loose – all without the Spirit leading us! But when the Holy Spirit leads us great victories can be achieved in the name of Jesus!

"I was serving the Lord on a mission and in the morning in prayer, I saw a three-arched bridge in an inner vision," said a disciple of the Lord. "Later that day I was driving and I saw the same bridge I had seen in the vision. Suddenly, in the Spirit I saw a large dark figure standing on top of the bridge (Revelation 4:2). He was an enormous demonic being, a stronghold, as mentioned in Ephesians 6:12. He was standing astride the bridge, with his hands on his hips and everything about his appearance said, 'I'm the boss here.' I asked the Holy Spirit, 'What is that?' The Spirit responded, 'His name is unbelief and you must command him to go in Jesus' name.' In obedience I declared, 'In the name of Jesus I command you to depart from here,' and in a lightning instant, the demonic spirit was gone. But suddenly doubts flooded my mind and I prayed, 'Holy Spirit would you please confirm to me, in a way I can understand, that what I just saw all took place.' As I drove over the bridge into the small community, I sat on a bench to read my Bible and three people came over to me and one asked, 'Is that the Bible you are reading? Are you a born again Christian? Can you explain to me how to become a born again Christian?' Through this experience the Holy Spirit was teaching me the reality of our spiritual battle, that demonic powers can have influence over homes, villages, towns, cities and nations etc. (Daniel 10:13, 2 Corinthians 4:4, Ephesians 2:2, 1 John 2:11). When the Holy Spirit directs, these demonic powers can be expelled in Jesus' name and when a spirit of unbelief has to go, people begin to believe in Jesus Christ!"

Churches, organisations and structures can also become defiled by denying the gifts of the Spirit, or by the sins that have been committed and not confessed within. An evil presence enters when the Spirit of Christ has been rejected by sin, because it is an insult to the Spirit of grace (Mark 16:17, 1 Corinthians 14:39, Hebrews 10:29).

Jesus should be our Lord and the Lord of our churches, and when we accept His Lordship, no other can take His place. Yet, if the will of the Holy Spirit is openly rejected and refuted, the spirit of antichrist can enter to replace the Spirit of Christ with religion (1 John 2:18, 22). John explained some believers in the early church rejected the revealed will of the Spirit of Christ (1 Peter 1:11), and became enslaved by the antichrist spirit (1 John 2:18-19).

If we are to understand the spiritual battle we are in, it is the Holy Spirit and He alone who can guide us with His discernment. The gift of discernment from the Holy Spirit is the ability to know the difference between what is from God and what is from man, or the devil (1 Kings 22:19-23, Matthew 10:1, Mark 5:1-20, Luke 9:37-42, Acts 16:16-18). The Holy Spirit enables the individual to 'see' or 'know' what is not from God and what source it originates from.

Jesus knew the secrets of men's hearts by the gift of discernment: 'Jesus perceived in His spirit that they reasoned thus within themselves, He said to them, "Why do you reason about these things in your hearts?" ' (Mark 2:8). God always has the mastery over all demonic beings. "I will send a spirit upon him, and he shall hear a rumour and return to his own land" (2 Kings 19:7).

Through Jesus' experiences we also find that many other evil spirits are at work in the world and He defeated them all. 'He cured many of infirmities, afflictions and evil spirits' (Luke 7:21).

The apostles also confronted evil spirits: 'The diseases left them and the evil spirits went out of them' (Acts 19:12). In the Bible we learn that demonic beings are real, with personalities and they can speak through people: 'The evil spirit answered and said, "Jesus I know and Paul I know; but who are you?" ' (Acts 19:15). Job also understood that demonic beings can speak through people: 'And whose spirit spoke through you?' (Job 26:4). John warned: 'Beloved, do not believe every spirit, but test the spirits, whether they are of God' (1 John 4:1).

In the Bible we are told many times that God does not want us to be ignorant and all He has revealed to us through Scripture is for our spiritual education. 'For whatever things were written before were written for our learning' (Roman 15:4).

In the Bible God reveals the names of many demonic beings. A spirit of jealousy (Numbers 5:14), familiar spirit (1 Samuel 28:7), lying spirit (1 Kings 22:22), spirit of haughtiness (Proverbs 16:18-19), perverse spirit (Isaiah 19:14), spirit of slumber (Isaiah 29:10, Romans 11:8), spirit of heaviness (Isaiah 61:3), spirit of harlotry (Hosea 5:4), foul spirit (Mark 9:25), spirit of infirmity (Luke 13:10), deaf and dumb spirit (Mark 9:17-29), spirit of divination (Acts 16:16), spirit of bondage (Romans 8:15), spirit of the world (1 Corinthians 2:12), spirit of death (1 Corinthians 10:10, 15:26), seducing spirit (1 Timothy 4:1), spirit of fear (2 Timothy 1:7), spirit of antichrist (1 John 4:3), and the spirit of error (1 John 4:6).

The Bible teaches there are many names and titles for demons, and we can expect the Spirit to reveal other names of demonic beings whom He is binding in His intercession. But before the Lord will lead us to pray big prayers to change nations, we will first have to deal with 'little devils.'

Where did these demons come from? The answer is found in the Bible. We learn that God created the heavens and the earth (Colossians 1:16, Hebrews 1:2). Earth became mankind's domain and in heaven God created endless numbers of angels, with a hierarchical structure. The most powerful of these angels were three archangels – Michael, Gabriel and Lucifer. The third angel rebelled and was cast out of heaven (Luke 10:18), and it was he, through his sin that became the devil (Ezekiel 28:12-17, Isaiah 14:12-15). But he did not fall alone, for he took with him one third of the angels, who became his demons (Revelation 12:4-9). Jesus speaking of this said, "I saw Satan fall like lightning from heaven" (Luke 10:18), and He spoke of "the devil and his angels" (Matthew 25:41). For every demon in rebellion to God, there are still two angels in submission to Him! We should never be afraid of evil spirits, they should be afraid of us (Luke 10:20, James 2:19). Jesus said, "These signs will follow those who believe: In My name they will cast out demons...they will speak with new tongues" (Mark 16:17).

Much of what happens in this world goes on in the unseen realms as the 'whole world lies under the sway of the evil one' (1 John 5:19). Demons, also known as evil spirits are subservient to the devil, who seeks to kill, steal and destroy anyone and everyone (John 10:10). They too seek bodies in which to dwell (Luke 9:42).

Demons battle against our peace of mind and our physical well being, and generally try to harass or torment people (1 Samuel 16:14-16, Luke 13:11-13, 1 Peter 1:13). They can cause sickness (Luke 13:11, Mark 7:25, 9:17), inflict people, cause destruction (Job 1:13-2:10), hinder conversions (Mark 4:15, 2 Corinthians 4:3-4), and plant evil desires (1 Chronicles 21:1). Demons can operate from within (Matthew 8:28-32), or outside of the human body (2 Corinthians 12:7). Demons can be cast out of people and off them – this is commonly known as deliverance. Jesus 'cast out demons by the Spirit of God' (Matthew 12:28), and so must His disciples.

Jesus told us that Satan, as a fallen angel, has come to "kill, steal and destroy" on earth (John 10:10). But Jesus came to deliver us from his evil power: 'God anointed Jesus of Nazareth with the Holy Spirit and with power, who went about doing good and healing all who were oppressed by the devil, for God was with Him' (Acts 10:38).

Casting demons out of people was a part of the ministry of Jesus and the apostles, and this power was given to all disciples of Jesus Christ in the Great Commission given by Jesus (Mark 16:17). However, some Christians get confused about deliverance because they misunderstand the teaching of the Bible and think that 'having a demon' means being totally possessed by devils. There is a huge difference between people who are totally possessed by demonic beings and people who are oppressed by demons. The Lord met a man who had lost control of himself and was totally possessed by a large number of demons called Legion (Matthew 8:28-33). But this is not the only teaching concerning demons in the Bible.

There are at least forty-four mentions of demons or devils in the New Testament. The Lord also exercised the ministry of deliverance to help Mary, out of whom He cast seven demons (Luke 8:2). She was not totally possessed by devils, but was oppressed with only seven demons that had to be cast out of her, and those with similar problems today can also be set free. People who are 'totally possessed' by a legion of devils are often the ones who have given themselves over to witchcraft and service of the devil. Casting out weak and insignificant demonic beings oppressing people was a regular feature in the ministry of the apostles and the Lord. However, we must not confuse the sins of the flesh (Galatians 5:19-21), with demonic oppression (Matthew 18:34, Ephesians 4:27, James 4:7, 2 Peter 2).

Christ defeated all demonic powers when He rose from the dead. Then He poured out His Spirit upon the Church. The deepest part of any human is his or her spirit and Job learned, 'The Spirit of God has made me and the breath of the Almighty gives me life' (Job 33:4). Through our actions, we can unite ourselves with the will of the Holy Spirit or with the will of evil spirits! Jesus said, "You do not know what manner of spirit you are of" (Luke 9:55).

"After I became a Christian I received deliverance from demons," said a disciple of the Lord. "It's clear from the teaching of Jesus that people cannot be delivered who refuse His Lordship, because the Holy Spirit must fill the areas the enemy leaves, or they will end up in a worst state then at the beginning (Luke 11:26). Many years later, I fell into sin again, and I tried to cast out the demons that I thought were making me sin and the Holy Spirit told me, 'You cannot cast self out of self.' The demons had already been cast out; self was now the problem and self must be crucified with Christ."

This is an example of the Holy Spirit revealing the truth of Scripture, because Christians are commanded to resist the devil and to stand firm against him, whilst wearing the full armour of God (1 Peter 5:8-9, Ephesians 6:10-17).

Christians have been given power and authority in the name of Jesus Christ the Lord to cast devils out or off people. Jesus Christ is the 'King of kings and the Lord of lords' (Revelation 19:16), and He came to 'destroy the works of the devil' (1 John 3:8). Jesus has broken Satan's authority and all demons are subject to Him (Philippians 2:10, Colossians 2:15, Hebrews 2:14, James 2:19). Jesus' authority has been passed onto disciples of Jesus Christ the Lord who are called to carry on His work in strict obedience to the Spirit (Matthew 10:8, 28:18-20). The Holy Spirit, who is in us, is stronger than the devil (1 John 4:4).

We can cast out devils at any time, but in greater spiritual warfare we cannot go to war with principalities and powers without the direct leading of our Great Commander. If we attempt to bind principalities and powers without the leading of God, we shall be like a soldier going absent without leave. The principle of obeying God's leading in warfare is made very clear in the account of Joshua's conquest of Canaan, and in the spiritual battles of the New Testament. 'Yet

Michael the archangel, in contending with the devil, when he disputed about the body of Moses, dared not bring against him a reviling accusation, but said, "The Lord rebuke you!" ' (Jude 9).

Satan's defeat was achieved with Christ's death and resurrection. Jesus 'having disarmed principalities and powers made a public spectacle of them, triumphing over them in it' (Colossians 2:15), and believers overcome 'by the blood of the Lamb...' (Revelation 12:11). This war is ongoing, but we know the end: 'The God of peace will crush Satan under your feet shortly' (Romans 16:20).

Satan is afraid that Christians will use the weapons God has given to them, so he does all he can to keep Christians in fear of spiritual warfare and deliverance, in order to protect his own kingdom (Luke 11:18). But if we live in Christ and abide in Him, there is no need for us ever to fear the enemy because we can live in His rest: 'The Spirit of the Lord causes him to rest' (Isaiah 63:14), and we live 'under the shadow of His wings,' as the manifold wisdom of God is 'made known by the Church to the principalities and powers in the heavenly places' (Ephesians 3:10).

In all warfare we can walk in the six-fold blessing of the presence of God. 'The Spirit of the Lord shall rest upon Him, the Spirit of wisdom and understanding, the Spirit of counsel and might, the Spirit of knowledge and of the fear of the Lord' (Isaiah 11:2). Jesus Christ needed all the attributes of the Holy Spirit to be at work in His ministry and so must we. We like Ezekiel will need to be led and guided by the Spirit: 'Then the Spirit entered me...' (Ezekiel 3:24).

Many Christian leaders spent decades receiving revelation from the Holy Spirit concerning the power of Christ to break all curses, heal the sick and cast out demons etc., in our day. Therefore, it would be very sad if we ignored all the Holy Spirit has taught them because of indifference or laziness. All we need to sacrifice is our pride and our time to read the books that they wrote concerning their lessons from God. These books are eye-opening: *Blessing or Curse: You can Choose* by Derek Prince, *Christian Set Yourself Free* by Graham and Shirley Powell, *Rees Howells Intercessor* by Norman Grubb, *Samuel Rees Howells: A Life of Intercession* by Richard Maton, *Revival Fires and Awakening* by Mathew Backholer and *Extreme Faith: On Fire Christianity* by Mathew Backholer.

*Questions to consider:* Christ commanded us to cast our demons, are you obeying Christ? Will you set aside time to read the books that will educate, inform and empower you?

*Actions:* Read the books mentioned above and learn from them.

# Chapter Forty

## Victory Over Death

### Jesus Raised from the Dead by the Holy Spirit and Father

- '…and declared to be the Son of God with power according to the Spirit of holiness, by the resurrection from the dead' (Romans 1:4).
- 'If the Spirit of Him who raised Jesus from the dead dwells in you, He who raised Christ from the dead will also give life to your mortal bodies through His Spirit who dwells in you' (Romans 8:11).
- 'Jesus Christ and God the Father who raised Him from the dead' (Galatians 1:1).
- 'The God of our Lord Jesus Christ, the Father of glory, may give to you the spirit of wisdom and revelation in the knowledge of Him…according to the working of His mighty power which He worked in Christ when He raised Him from the dead' (Ephesians 1:17, 20).
- 'For Christ also suffered once for sins, the just for the unjust, that He might bring us to God, being put to death in the flesh but made alive by the Spirit' (1 Peter 3:18-19).

### Put to Death the Deeds of the Body

- 'For if you live according to the flesh you will die; but if by the Spirit you put to death the deeds of the body, you will live. For as many as are led by the Spirit of God, these are sons of God. For you did not receive the spirit of bondage again to fear, but you received the Spirit of adoption by whom we cry out, "Abba, Father." The Spirit Himself bears witness with our spirit that we are children of God' (Romans 8:13-16).
- Jesus said, "He who has an ear, let him hear what the Spirit says to the churches. He who overcomes shall not be hurt by the second death" (Revelation 2:11).

### In the Spirit

- 'In the Spirit…' (Romans 8:9).
- 'The Spirit of God…' (Romans 8:9).
- 'The Spirit of Christ…' (Romans 8:9).

# Chapter Forty-One

## The Holy Spirit and the Plan of God

Samuel Rees Howells taught every generation of students at the Bible College that his father founded, that the Holy Spirit is ever seeking human vessels through whom He can live and work. Samuel explained that in each and every generation, the Holy Spirit seeks out those who will surrender all to Jesus and allow Him to live His Divine life through them. When the Holy Spirit finds men and women who will meet this calibre of surrender, this will begin a process which transforms the individual, but also prepares him or her to be a channel of God's blessing to the world.

In 1910, R.A. Torrey wrote: 'It is one thing to have the Holy Spirit dwelling way back in the consciousness, in some hidden sanctuary of the being, and something quite different and vastly more, to have Him take possession of the whole house that He inhabits!'[1]

The baptism of fire is all consuming. It means allowing God into every area of your being and letting His fire burn out sin, selfishness and empty desire. We see this taking place in many of the lives of people in the Bible. The experience is different for all and ongoing, but the outcome the same. God ends up in charge and the person becomes His servant.

God's search for human vessels through whom He can work in the world is a continual theme throughout the entire Bible. Therefore if you have ever thought that the Holy Spirit was not at work in the Old Testament, then you have been misinformed because the Holy Spirit was ministering in the lives of all those called by God, just as the New Testament confirms. It was the Holy Spirit who wrote the Old Testament through the lives of those who obeyed God. 'No prophecy of Scripture is of any private interpretation, for prophecy never came by the will of man, but holy men of God spoke as they were moved by the Holy Spirit' (2 Peter 1:20-21).

The plan of God for world redemption has always been ushered forward by men and women who were filled and led by the Spirit of God. When God finds a person who will invite the Holy Spirit into his or her life in all His fullness, Paul explained what will happen next: 'That you may be filled with the fullness of God. Now to Him who is able to do exceeding abundantly above all we ask or think, according to the power that works in us' (Ephesians 3:19-20). The measure of the power that will be released through us, is the measure to which the Power works in us. It is this path that leads us to do exceeding abundantly above all we can ask or think, because it is not us who asks, or who does, but the Spirit within us. This was the case in the lives of Old Testament characters and in the New.

In the years 1924-1950, Rees Howells went through the Scriptures with staff and students at his Bible College and revisited the lives of the servants of God whom the Holy Spirit had entered to use for His purposes. Then from 1950-2002, Samuel Rees Howells followed the same path, as Samuel taught on Gideon, Paul, John and others from the Bible, who the Holy Spirit clothed Himself with. What was evident in all they taught, was that the Spirit of God has always been and will always be central to the plan of God being outworked in the world.

The lives of all the biblical characters, we are told, are recorded as examples to us for a witness and warning: 'For whatever things were written before were written for our learning, that we through the patience and comfort of the Scriptures might have hope' (Romans 15:4). This message is repeated several times in the Bible (Romans 4:23-25, 1 Corinthians 10:11, 2 Timothy 3:16-17). We can all learn much about the work of the Spirit in the Old Testament.

In the first verse of the Bible we are introduced to God the Father, the Creator of all. In the second verse we are introduced to the Holy Spirit. 'The Spirit of God was hovering over the face of the waters' (Genesis 1:2). John describing the very same events explains how Jesus, the Word, was also there in the eternal realm (Micah 5:2, John 1:1-4, 14, Colossians 1:15-17, 1 John 1:1, Revelation 19:13). Together, the three members of the Trinity decided, "Let Us make man in Our image" (Genesis 1:26, Colossians 1:16). Therefore, God the Father, God the Son and God the Holy Spirit worked together in creation (Genesis 1:2, Job 26:13, 33:4, Psalm 104:30). Thus, we learn the Bible begins with the Holy Spirit and the Father, and it also ends with the Holy Spirit glorifying the Son, 'and the Spirit and the Bride say, "Come!" ' (Revelation 22:17).

After the fall of mankind (Genesis 2:17, 3:8-24, Romans 3:23, 1 Corinthians 15:22), God commenced His predetermined plan of mankind's redemption (Matthew 25:34, Ephesians 1:4, 1 Peter 1:20, Revelation 13:8), as He laid the foundations for the nation of Israel. He called Abraham and his sons, and gave them a progressive revelation of Himself and to all the patriarchs and prophets who would follow. All were dependent on the revelation of the Holy Spirit (1 Peter 1:11). Through these patriarchs and prophets God revealed His character and foretold that God Himself would come to earth in Christ, to be the Saviour of all who believe in Him (Isaiah 9:6).

To prepare the people called Israel, through whom the Saviour would come, God drew ancient Israel and made them into one people. Using His servant Joseph, God saved Israel from famine, and drew them to Egypt. God gave Joseph the ability to exercise several gifts of the Spirit. He had supernatural wisdom, could see the 'big' picture and he interpreted dreams because he was filled with God's Spirit (Genesis 31:3). Pharaoh recognised the Divine Presence working in Joseph's life and Daniel later had a similar experience (Daniel 4:8-9).

To deliver the people of Israel from Egypt, God raised up Moses and filled him with the Spirit (Numbers 11:24-29). When Israel left Egypt through the wilderness route, the Holy Spirit was with them. 'As the Holy Spirit says, "Today, if you will hear His voice, do not harden your hearts as in the rebellion, in the day of trial in the wilderness, where your fathers tested Me, tried Me..." ' (Hebrews 3:7-11).

To help make them into a unique nation, God chose a man to make all the holy items for use in worship. "I have filled him with the Spirit of God in wisdom, in understanding, in knowledge and in all manner of workmanship" (Exodus 31:3). We learn that the Holy Spirit builds God's tabernacle in and through His anointed vessels.

In the book of Numbers we find it was the Holy Spirit who inspired and anointed Moses to give the law to the people, so that they would be a nation governed by the rule of God's law (Numbers 11:17). The Holy Spirit directed to Moses the plan of the Tabernacle and by doing so, He also left a legacy to us about the importance of the layout of the Tabernacle in the purposes of God (Hebrews 9:8).

One of the important directions the Spirit gave to Moses about the establishment of the Kingdom of Israel, with its holy priesthood, was to decree that every leader, King and priest should be anointed with oil (Exodus 29:4-7, 1 Samuel 16:13). The oil represents the anointing of the Holy Spirit for ministry. The Holy Spirit was given to all the leaders in ancient Israel to instruct them in the ways of God (Nehemiah 9:20). However, if Israel was to be the true people of God, all their leaders would need to be filled and guided by the Holy Spirit, and the Spirit was given to all the leaders under Moses, and they prophesied (Numbers 11:17, 25-26).

When the Spirit was poured out on all the elders, young Joshua was concerned for Moses' role as prophet and asked Moses to "forbid them." Moses had discovered that the work of God only progresses when the Holy Spirit finds suitable human vessels, through whom He can work, and so Moses declared, "Oh that all the Lord's people were prophets and that the Lord would put His Spirit upon them!" (Numbers 11:29).

The children of Israel were now one nation, with distinct laws and one God. Now they needed a land of their own and the Holy Spirit came upon Joshua to prepare him to take the nation into the Promised Land. 'The Lord said to Moses, "Take Joshua the son of Nun with you, a man in whom is the Spirit" ' (Numbers 27:18).

After the conquest of Canaan was complete, and Joshua and all from his generation died, the children of Israel did not have any leaders who were filled with God's Spirit. The nation had backslid and each person did what was right in his or her own eyes (Judges 17:6). To reform the nation the Holy Spirit sought out willing vessels to lead and direct, to save Israel from oppression, and bring them back to the Lord in true worship.

We learn this lesson from Israel's experience: Any work that God begins by the leading of the Holy Spirit can only be continued by people who have received and know the Spirit; these people must have paid the same price of the pioneers of the past and matched the calibre of surrender of previous generations.

To help restore the people, God first found Ehud and 'the Spirit of the Lord came upon him' (Judges 3:10), then later the Spirit took possession of Gideon (Judges 6:34). To prove that the hand of flesh can never fulfil the purposes of God, and to indicate all of mankind's great ideas and strength are insufficient, the Lord led Gideon to save the nation by only three hundred men: 'The people who are with you are too many for Me to give the Midianites into their hands, lest Israel claim glory for itself against Me, saying, "My own hand has saved me" ' (Judges 7:2). Thus pride, self-reliance and self-belief are a great hinderance to the work of the Spirit. If we believe 'we can do this,' and 'we have all we need,' we will fail miserably. Rees Howells taught that "man's extremity is God's opportunity."

Every time the Holy Spirit found a vessel who would obey the Lord's will in the book of Judges, the nation of Israel was delivered, but after they found relief again, they soon backslid away from God and fell into bondage again. The same experience is witnessed in the lives of millions today who receive the blessing of the Spirit, but after finding relief in the peace of Jesus Christ, they go back to the old ways. It is a very dangerous thing to become 'partakers of the Holy Spirit' and return back to the world, for it is an insult to 'the Spirit of grace' (Hebrews 6:4-6, 10:29).

As Israel backslid, the Holy Spirit sought another person through whom He could work and He found Jephthah. Moses had been set apart by birth for God to use him, Joshua had been trained by Moses in his school of living faith, but Jephthah was the son of a prostitute, an outcast, a man with a sordid background who grew up on the wrong side of town; yet God chose him.

Jephthah was angered by the way he had been rejected because of the sins of his parents, and he was expelled from his people, lost his inheritance and became a leader of worthless men (Judges 11:1-11). Nonetheless, we learn from his life that the Lord does not hold anyone's past against them and the Holy Spirit will find His vessels from any place or family He chooses. "Can anything good come out of Nazareth?…Come and see" (John 1:46). It's not where you've come from that concerns God, but where you're going, and how much you are prepared to sacrifice and obey.

We learn from the Bible that Jephthah knew the history of God's dealings with Israel, he believed in the Lord's powerful judgment, in His righteousness and he was a man who kept his vows to God, even if he did not understand that God never asks for the kind of sacrifice that he gave (Judges 11:15-24, 27, 39, Jeremiah 19:5).

Jephthah operated in the light he had received up until that point in his life and God knew his heart was right. In the words of Rees Howells he was "willing to be made willing" to be a vessel of the Lord and 'the Spirit of the Lord came upon Jephthah' (Judges 11:29). Israel was saved again and the Lord was honoured.

Israel again did evil in the sight of the Lord and the Holy Spirit began to come upon a man, who teaches us that the anointing of God does not constitute His favour with people's behaviour, as 'the gifts and the calling of God are irrevocable' (Romans 11:29).

Samson was a man who never learnt to crucify the flesh, and when the Holy Spirit is not welcomed to deal with the inner self, that selfish root inside of us can destroy all God has been working to achieve through us. It takes a powerful anointing to accomplish the will of God, but it takes true character to keep us where God will put us (Romans 5:4). Nevertheless, 'The Spirit of God came mightily upon him' (Judges 14:6), and on his own, Samson tore a lion apart in preparation for future battles with the enemy. In this secret battle away from public view, Samson learnt that the Spirit could empower him for service. 'Then the Spirit of the Lord came upon him mightily,' and his power, once tested in the secret place, was manifested publicly as he killed thirty enemies of God's people (Judges 14:9).

The private demonstration of the power of the Holy Spirit upon him prepared him to go out into the public and battle God's enemies. 'Then the Spirit of the Lord came mightily upon him' and he killed a thousand of God's enemies (Judges 15:14).

Satan knew he could not empower his servants on earth to be stronger than the Spirit in Samson, so instead he sought out Samson's area of greatest vulnerability and the enemy used Delilah to lull him to sleep on her knees (Judges 16:19).

When the Holy Spirit was upon Samson, no-one could defeat him, but as the Spirit had never been welcomed by him to deal with his flesh life, he could not discern the enemy in Delilah and was rendered powerless by an evil woman's deception. Nevertheless, after Samson had been humiliated and defeated, he repented and turned back to God in full faith. Then, in a last stand of sacrifice, Samson laid his life on the altar as he cried out in faith, "O Lord God, remember me I pray! Strengthen me, I pray just this once" (Judges 16:28). Samson had sinned many times, but in his death he brought about a great victory over Israel's enemies (Judges 16:28-31).

Why did the Holy Spirit come upon sinful Samson? Perhaps the Lord wanted us to learn from Samson's life that even if we accomplish much for Him, if we do not develop a true holy character, we will always reap what we sow (Psalm 126:5, Hosea 10:12). 'Do not be deceived, God is not mocked; for whatever a man sows, that he will also reap' (Galatians 6:7).

One lesson from Samson's life is that sometimes due to the grace of God the Spirit will come upon sinful men and even unbelievers for His purposes (Numbers 24:1-2); and it remains a warning to us, that God's power does not indicate His favour with our lifestyles.

This theme is echoed by the first King of Israel. Saul became the first king, but he needed a supernatural touch from the Holy Spirit to prepare him for the work. Samuel said, 'The Spirit of the Lord will come upon you, and you will prophesy with them and be turned into another man. So it was, when he had turned his back to go from Samuel that God gave him another heart; and all those signs came to pass that day. When they came there to the hill, there was a group of prophets to meet him; then the Spirit of God came upon him, and he prophesied among them' (1 Samuel 10:6, 9-10).

To prepare King Saul to deliver Israel from her enemies and in order for the people to worship God in peace, the Holy Spirit would stir up righteous anger in Saul. 'Then the Spirit of God came upon Saul when he heard this news and his anger was greatly aroused' (1 Samuel 11:6). We often think of the Spirit of peace, but He is also jealous and angry at sin (Genesis 6:3, Nahum 1:2, James 4:5).

When the Holy Spirit came upon Saul, he turned into another man and received a new heart from God. However, as Saul did not show true repentance for his mistakes and did not renew his mind, he turned back into the old Saul (Romans 12:2). The Spirit of God supernaturally transformed him, but his 'stinking thinking' gradually undid all God had achieved in him. We learn from this that if we don't allow the Holy Spirit to teach us to renew our minds, we also shall return to our old defeated state. We may receive a powerful touch from the Spirit of God, or a wonderful baptism of grace, but unless we agree to allow God to make that change permanent in us, our flesh life will repossess the land the Spirit now possesses!

Due to his disobedience, King Saul was rejected as leader of the nation and the Lord sought out a new king for Israel. The Holy Spirit found David, a man after God's own heart. 'Then Samuel took the horn of oil and anointed him in the midst of his brothers; and the Spirit of the Lord came upon David from that day forward' (1 Samuel 16:13).

David was anointed by the Holy Spirit to become king; meanwhile Saul was still in power. We learn that positions of power, titles and hieratical structures can never replace the call of the Spirit, and it is possible to have the title, but not the call or anointing.

Saul's disobedience provides us with a solemn warning – if we disobey God, His Presence can leave us, even if we are still in a powerful leadership position. 'So Samuel arose and went to Ramah. But the Spirit of the Lord departed from Saul, and a distressing spirit from the Lord troubled him' (1 Samuel 16:14). Saul became like Samson who 'did not know that the Lord had departed from him' (Judges 16:20). Saul never learnt to abide in the Spirit of God and he never became sensitive to the Spirit. He chose not to learn how to make his body, a home fit for the Spirit (1 Corinthians 6:18-20).

As Saul maintained a life of disobedience, he fell further away from the grace of God and his heart was hardened. He sought to kill David, but God intervened to protect the future king of Israel. 'Then Saul sent messengers to take David. And when they saw the group of prophets prophesying and Samuel standing as leader over them, the Spirit of God came upon the messengers of Saul, and they also prophesied. And when Saul was told, he sent other messengers and they prophesied likewise. Saul sent messengers again the third time and they prophesied also...Then the Spirit of God was upon him also, and he went on and prophesied' (1 Samuel 19:20-23).

David learnt to work with the anointing of the Holy Spirit upon his life and after countless years of trials, he became king and could testify, "The Spirit of the Lord spoke by me and His Word was on my tongue" (2 Samuel 23:2).

David learnt how to let the Holy Spirit speak through him, as Jesus noted, "How then does David in the Spirit call Him 'Lord?' " (Matthew 22:43). The apostles confirmed this, "Men and brethren, this Scripture had to be fulfilled, which the Holy Spirit spoke before by the mouth of David" (Acts 1:16). Later the apostles also learnt to let the Spirit speak through them, 'They were not able to resist the wisdom and the Spirit by which he spoke' (Acts 6:10). Peter acknowledged this truth and wrote: 'If anyone speaks, let him speak as the oracles of God' (1 Peter 4:11).

Nevertheless, instead of focusing on the ministry God had given to David, he began to get complacent about his call. When it was time for king's to go out to battle, Satan lured David into sin through complacency (2 Samuel 11:1-27). After committing adultery and murder, David realised he could lose the precious Presence and anointing of God and cried out, "Do not cast me away from Your Presence and do not take Your Holy Spirit from me" (Psalm 51:11).

When King Saul sinned, he did not display any true inner repentance and he lost God's blessing. But King David, after being confronted by Nathan the prophet, was led into a time of great purging repentance. Through this, King David found that God has great mercy for humble and repentant sinners, who have broken and contrite spirits. God loves restoration. 'The sacrifices of God are a broken spirit, a broken and a contrite heart – these, O God, You will not despise' (Psalm 51:17).

King David is remembered as a great king because he had a repentant humble heart and he acknowledged his need for the Holy Spirit. In the book of Psalms, we learn that David had a deep understanding of the work of the Spirit of God: 'Where can I go from Your Spirit? Or where can I flee from Your presence?' (Psalm 139:7). He knew the Holy Spirit could be with him at all times and that the Spirit would teach him to do the will of God, leading Him to righteousness: 'Teach me to do Your will, for You are my God; Your Spirit is good. Lead me in the land of uprightness' (Psalm 143:10).

After King David, came his son Solomon and the Kingdom was divided after Solomon's death. From then on, there were many kings over Israel and Judah, but many of them did not follow the Lord. Then God raised up Elijah the prophet, who walked closely with God and called fire down from heaven, to get backslidden Israel to confront reality. He walked so close with God, that the Spirit could physically transport him from one place to another (1 Kings 18:36-39). 'And it shall come to pass, as soon as I am gone from you, that the Spirit of the Lord will carry you to a place I do not know' (1 Kings 18:12). When his ministry was complete, he was taken to heaven, without tasting death and the young prophets said, "Look now, there are fifty strong men with your servants. Please let them go and search for your master, lest perhaps the Spirit of the Lord has taken him up and cast him upon some mountain or into some valley" (2 Kings 2:16). The prophet Ezekiel was also moved in the Spirit: 'The Spirit lifted me up and brought me into the inner court; and behold, the glory of the Lord filled the temple' (Ezekiel 43:5), and so did Philip. 'Now when they came up out of the water, the Spirit of the Lord caught Philip away, so that the eunuch saw him no more; and he went on his way rejoicing' (Acts 8:39).

Before Elijah was taken away by God, the Lord led him to find Elisha, his young successor, and this man had a choice to make. Rees Howells would often cite Elisha as an example of the cost of following the Holy Spirit unconditionally. When the call came, Elisha had to decide if he was willing to give up everything to follow the Lord. Elisha 'burnt-up' his old life and followed the Lord with his whole heart (1 Kings 19:19-21). It was this willingness to lay all on the altar of the Lord that gave him the authority to ask for an outstanding anointing. 'Elijah said to Elisha, "Ask, what may I do for you, before I am taken away from you?" Elisha said, "Please let a double portion of your spirit be upon me" ' (2 Kings 2:9).

Elisha paid the same price of total abandonment to the Lord as Elijah and the Bible documents his miraculous ministry was double that of his mentor, and the school of the prophets recognised it was the Holy Spirit upon him that did the great works. 'Now when the sons of the prophets who were from Jericho saw him, they said,

"The spirit of Elijah rests on Elisha" ' (2 Kings 2:15).

When reaching out to the non-believing nations around Israel, God proved His deep concern that His great name should be glorified and never tainted by the greed of man (Matthew 11:7-9). When Naaman the Syrian came to Israel to seek healing from the true God, Elisha was used as a channel to tell him how God would heal him. To prove that he was a real man of God and not a greedy false prophet, he refused any gift from the Syrian. This powerful witness of the God who heals and a prophet who seeks no reward was to be a wonderful testimony to the people of Syria. Nonetheless, Elisha's servant Gehazi was tainted with greed and made up a lie, which suggested the God of Israel could not provide (2 Kings 5:16-27). Thus the testimony of healing was tainted as Gehazi secretly sought payment from Naaman. Nevertheless, the Spirit gave Elisha special discernment and he said the Gehazi, "Did not my heart go with you when the man turned back from his chariot to meet you? Is it time to receive money and to receive clothing, olive groves and vineyards, sheep and oxen, male and female servants?" (2 Kings 5:26). The Spirit was grieved (Isaiah 63:10), and Gehazi was judged by God (2 Kings 5:27). The spirit of greed and the Spirit of God do not abide together. A true prophet does not lust after profit (Luke 12:34).

The Lord sent many other prophets to the people of Israel and Judah, who spoke by the Holy Spirit, but they refused to listen to Him: "The Holy Spirit spoke rightly through Isaiah the prophet to our fathers," testified Paul (Acts 28:25). All the prophets spoke as they were moved by the Spirit of God (Nehemiah 9:30). 'For prophecy never came by the will of man, but holy men of God spoke as they were moved by the Holy Spirit' (2 Peter 1:21).

Jeremiah warned God's people of their coming captivity if they refused to listen to the Holy Spirit who spoke through him (Hebrews 10:15-16), but they would not heed and Isaiah's prophecy was fulfilled: "Go and tell this people, 'Keep on hearing, but do not understand; keep on seeing, but do not perceive.' Make the heart of this people dull, and their ears heavy, and shut their eyes; lest they see with their eyes, and hear with their ears and understand with their heart, and return and be healed" ' (Isaiah 6:9-10). One of their judgments was to be the victim of their own self-delusion (Isaiah 66:4, Matthew 15:14, Romans 1:24-27).

The great problem with the people of Israel was their hearts were divided. They wanted the best of the Lord, but they also wanted sin. One disciple of the Lord was seeking the Lord when God spoke to him saying, "Your heart is divided. You state that you have given your heart to the Lord, but in truth you have only given part of your heart to Me." How many people today are like the people of ancient Israel? How many of our hearts are divided between wanting to walk with God, whilst loving this world, consumerism, anger, greed, pride, lust and selfish ambition, etc?

This is the very reason why God wants all of us to have a Holy Spirit heart transplant: 'I will give you a new heart and put a new spirit within you; I will take the heart of stone out of your flesh and give you a heart of flesh. I will put My Spirit within you and cause you to walk in My statutes, and you will keep My judgments and do them' (Ezekiel 36:26-27).

The Spirit of God rested on the prophets and the Spirit of Christ testified of the Saviour's coming (Ephesians 3:5-6), and He revealed in part, God's plan of salvation: 'Of this salvation the prophets have inquired and searched carefully, who prophesied of the grace that would come to you, searching what, or what manner of time, the Spirit of Christ who was in them, was indicating when He testified beforehand the sufferings of Christ and the glories that would follow. To them it was revealed that, not to themselves, but to us they were ministering the things which now have been reported to you through those who have preached the gospel to you by the Spirit sent from heaven – things which angels desire to look into' (1 Peter 1:10-12).

When Christ came to earth, every aspect of His ministry was guided by the Holy Spirit and after His death, resurrection and ascension into heaven, God poured out His Holy Spirit to birth the Church, in fulfilment of Joel's prophecy: 'And it shall come to pass afterward that I will pour out My Spirit on all flesh; Your sons and your daughters shall prophesy, your old men shall dream dreams, your young men shall see visions. And also on My menservants and on My maidservants, I will pour out My Spirit in those days' (Joel 2:28-29). The apostles were filled, led and guided by the Spirit and they learnt to be sensitive to His voice in all things. As they surrendered to the Lord Jesus, it was the Holy Spirit who filled them, and they learnt one great secret: only the Holy Spirit can make Jesus the Lord of someone's life, and they left us with this testimony to inspire, encourage and challenge: 'No one can say, "Jesus is Lord," except by the Holy Spirit' (1 Corinthians 12:3).

*Questions to consider:* Do you understand how the plan of God unfolded in the Old Testament? Are you also led by the Holy Spirit?

*Actions:* Ask the Lord to fulfil His plan in your life by becoming a vessel given over to the Spirit. Seek Him today!

# Chapter Forty-Two

## The Spirit in Revelation

- 'I was in the Spirit on the Lord's Day' (Revelation 1:10).
- Jesus said, "Whoever has ears, let them hear what the Spirit says to the churches" (Revelation 2:7).
- Jesus said, "Whoever has ears, let them hear what the Spirit says to the churches" (Revelation 2:17).
- Jesus said, "Whoever has ears, let them hear what the Spirit says to the churches" (Revelation 2:29).
- Jesus said, "Whoever has ears, let them hear what the Spirit says to the churches" (Revelation 3:6).
- Jesus said, "Whoever has ears, let them hear what the Spirit says to the churches" (Revelation 3:13).
- Jesus said, "Whoever has ears, let them hear what the Spirit says to the churches" (Revelation 3:22).
- 'Immediately I was in the Spirit and behold, a throne set in heaven and One sat on the throne' (Revelation 4:2).
- 'From the throne proceeded lightnings, thunderings and voices. Seven lamps of fire were burning before the throne, which are the seven Spirits of God'...'The Spirit of the Lord (1) will rest on Him, the Spirit of Wisdom (2), and of Understanding (3), the Spirit of Counsel (4) and of Might (5), the Spirit of the Knowledge (6) and of the Fear of the Lord (7)' (Revelation 4:5, Isaiah 11:1-2).
- 'I heard a voice from heaven say, "Write this: Blessed are the dead who die in the Lord from now on." "Yes," says the Spirit, "they will rest from their labour, for their deeds will follow them" ' (Revelation 14:13).
- 'So he carried me away in the Spirit into the wilderness and I saw a woman sitting on a scarlet beast which was full of names of blasphemy, having seven heads and ten horns' (Revelation 17:3).
- "I am your fellow servant, and of your brethren who have the testimony of Jesus. Worship God! For the testimony of Jesus is the spirit of prophecy" (Revelation 19:10).
- 'He carried me away in the Spirit to a mountain great and high' (Revelation 21:10).
- 'The Spirit and the bride say, "Come!" ' (Revelation 22:17).

# Chapter Forty-Three

## Channels of the Holy Spirit

"He who does not know God the Holy Ghost, does not know God at all," preached Thomas Arnold (1795-1842), in a famous sermon. "We must pray then for the Spirit – the Spirit of holiness, the Spirit of liberty, the Spirit of peace, love and joy. As the apostles were changed by Him, so shall we."[1]

"There must be more," has been the heart-cry of millions of believers over the years, as they struggle with the shallowness of what has become 'normal Christianity.' "Did God save me to warm this pew every Sunday?" some ask and, "Is there a deeper experience with the Holy Spirit, than just seeking my own blessing?"

Some Christians have even stated that their churches appear to be having 'reruns' of services of yesteryear on autopilot, as they follow a routine, pattern and schedule – all devoid of power.

Many Christians who have testified to "being filled with the Holy Spirit," are so desperate for God, that they have travelled the world to be in 'the place' where God is moving. This is a very good thing, because it reveals their hunger; nevertheless, let's be very honest here, and I write as one who has travelled the world, if we were truly 'filled' with the Holy Spirit, would we need to travel so far to get 'another touch' of His presence and power? If He truly filled us and lived in us, in the same way He lived in others from previous generations, we would already be abiding in Him – in His power, in His presence and in His glory. We would not need to search for Him, because we would have already found Him!

Why do so many travel thousands of miles to find Him, whilst still claiming they are already 'filled' with Him? This seeking, desiring and craving for Him is a good sign that there is much more. However, we will not find an intimate relationship with the Holy Spirit by seeking out the latest wonderful 'portal,' or by trying to catch or receive the impartation of someone else's anointing, but by walking up to our Mount Moriah, where Abraham and David laid their costly sacrifices (Genesis 22:2-14, 2 Chronicles 3:1). Like Elijah, we have to rebuild the altar of the Lord before the fire will fall (1 Kings 18:30-39), and like Elisha, we too will have to pay the same price as our predecessors, if we wish to walk in the same anointing as they did.

There are many who have walked this path in the past like D.L. Moody, Rees Howells, Evan Roberts, Duncan Campbell and Samuel Rees Howells to name just five; all became channels of

God's power in their generation. What was their secret? The power which flowed through them was measured to their relationship with Christ and obedience to the Spirit of Christ. They did not have power to use as they wished at anytime, it was the Holy Spirit who led them into His work, and His power was manifested in His way, at His time, and always subject to His guidance.

Rees Howells was a man who knew how to prevail in intercession and he was a channel for God's blessing to the world. The secret to the powerful ministry Rees Howells exercised was that it was not him serving the Lord, but the Holy Spirit living in and through him.

The Holy Spirit revealed to Rees, "As the Saviour had a body, so I dwell in the cleansed temple of believers. I am a Person. I am God and I have come to ask you to give your body to Me that I may work through it. I need a body for My temple, but it must belong to Me without reserve, for two persons with different wills can never live in the same body. Will you give Me yours? But if I come in, I come as God and you must go out; I shall not mix Myself with your self" (Romans 12:1, 1 Corinthians 6:19, Colossians 3:2-3).

Rees Howells chose to surrender all to the Lord and gave himself unreservedly to God, and the Holy Spirit entered him and filled him. It was after this experience that the words of Jesus Christ came alive to him. "I tell you the truth. It is to your advantage that I go away; for if I do not go away, the Helper will not come to you; but if I depart, I will send Him to you" (John 16:7).

After Jesus' death, resurrection and ascension into heaven, the Holy Spirit was poured out to continue the ministry of Jesus on earth. That ministry, Jesus promised, would include the "greater works" of the Kingdom. "Most assuredly I say to you, he who believes in Me, the works that I do, he will do also and greater works than these he will do because I go to My Father" (John 14:12). Rees Howells witnessed these greater works, especially as this promise is connected to the life of prayer and intercession (John 14:12-14).

Jesus taught we would need the Holy Spirit to guide us into all truth and that the Spirit would speak the very words of Jesus to us, because the Spirit of God will take what belongs to Jesus and declare it to us. "When He the Spirit of Truth has come, He will guide you into all truth; for He will not speak on His own authority but whatever He hears He will speak and He will tell you things to come. He will glorify Me, for He will take what is Mine and declare it to you. All things that the Father has are Mine. Therefore I said that He will take of Mine and declare it to you" (John 16:13-15).

The Holy Spirit lives in unity with the Father and the Son. Jesus explained that the Holy Spirit speaks to us, "Whatever He hears" (John 16:13), and Jesus testified that, "Whatever I speak, just as the Father has told Me, so I speak" (John 12:50). Therefore, when we are led by the Spirit, we are also led by the Father and the Son!

We may declare that we love Jesus in heaven, but the ministry of Jesus continues in our lives and in the world, through the ministry of the Holy Spirit working in and through us! Why then are churches so often strangers to the ways, voice and will of the Holy Spirit? "The Church knows more about the Saviour, who was only on the earth thirty-three years," said Rees Howells, "than about the Holy Spirit who has been here two thousand years" (Revelation 2:17, 2:29, 3:6, 3:13, 3:22).

Perhaps two of the great sins of the Church today are indifference to God's revealed will and presumptuous service 'for Him.' Why are we trying to do His work, without God the Holy Spirit?

God has already warned His children of the great sin of trying to 'do works' for Him, without the direct leading, and guidance of the Holy Spirit. "Woe to the rebellious children," says the Lord, "who take counsel, but not of Me and who devise plans, but not of My Spirit, that they may add sin to sin" (Isaiah 30:1). If our works don't find their genesis in Him, then it is not God doing it, but us! Jesus warned, "The flesh profits nothing," because "it is the Spirit who gives life" (John 6:63).

"Most Christians, including Charismatic and Pentecostals, live in a world of massive spiritual contradictions," said a disciple of the Lord. "They choose to remain ignorant of the 'ifs' and 'buts' of Scripture, and believe they can ignore the principles of God, whilst expecting to get the results of obedience. Therefore they expect mass healings, revivals and blessings, despite the fact they have not met any of the conditions. This leads to mass confusion in the pews – did God promise or not? God's faithfulness should never be questioned – it is our obedience which should be questioned!

"The Spirit will challenge all of our hypocrisy. He will not allow us to pray powerful prayers, whilst we ignore all the Scriptures which provide the basis for answer to prayer. We won't be able to pray for healing, if we know we are wilfully ignorant of the terms and conditions for healing etc. The Holy Spirit will reveal the 'ifs' and 'buts' of the Bible, and He will expect us to live up to His standards. He never lowers God's standards, He expects us to come up to them!"

*Questions to consider:* Are you a disciple of Jesus or just another 'Christian?' Do you want to go further with God?

*Actions:* Make a stand today and ask God to revive you!

# Chapter Forty-Four

## The Comforter and Multiplier

- 'Then the churches throughout all Judea, Galilee and Samaria had peace and were edified. And walking in the fear of the Lord and in the comfort of the Holy Spirit, they were multiplied' (Acts 9:31).
- 'Peter rose up and said, "Men and brethren, you know that a good while ago God chose among us, that by my mouth the Gentiles should hear the Word of the gospel and believe. So God, who knows the heart, acknowledged them by giving them the Holy Spirit, just as He did to us, and made no distinction between us and them, purifying their hearts by faith" ' (Acts 15:7-9).
- 'He gave me the priestly duty of proclaiming the gospel of God, so that the Gentiles might become an offering acceptable to God, sanctified by the Holy Spirit. Therefore I glory in Christ Jesus in my service to God. I will not venture to speak of anything except what Christ has accomplished through me in leading the Gentiles to obey God by what I have said and done, by the power of signs and wonders, through the power of the Spirit of God. So from Jerusalem all the way around to Illyricum, I have fully proclaimed the gospel of Christ' (Romans 15:16-19).
- 'I know that when I come to you, I will come in the full measure of the blessing of Christ. I urge you, brothers and sisters, by our Lord Jesus Christ and by the love of the Spirit, to join me in my struggle by praying to God for me' (Romans 15:29-30).
- 'You are an epistle of Christ, ministered by us, written not with ink but by the Spirit of the living God, not on tablets of stone but on tablets of flesh, that is, of the heart' (2 Corinthians 3:3).
- 'Because you are sons, God has sent forth the Spirit of His Son into your hearts, crying out, "Abba, Father!" ' (Galatians 4:6).
- 'Our gospel came to you not simply with words but also with power, with the Holy Spirit and deep conviction. You know how we lived among you for your sake. You became imitators of us and of the Lord, for you welcomed the message in the midst of severe suffering with the joy given by the Holy Spirit' (1 Thessalonians 1:5-6).

# Chapter Forty-Five

## The Six-Fold Witness of the Spirit

"It's amazing how long it takes for the Church to humble itself before the Lord and acknowledge we cannot live this life or complete Jesus' Great Commission without the Holy Spirit," said a disciple of the Lord. "We have all worked so hard, laboured so long and travailed with all our might, and seen so little fruit in our lives and in the harvest! It is always when we come to the end of self, when our best intentions and ideas have failed that we finally say, 'God we cannot do this, will you please come and do the work?' Then, He answers and says, 'I've waited so long to hear you acknowledge your need of Me! Stop striving in the flesh and let My Holy Spirit do His work through you!' "

"The great spiritual danger that confronts so many professing Christians is that they've become insensitive to the voice of God," said Derek Prince. "They may continue in their religious activities, but its all a ritual and formal, just a matter of a life pattern, and habits they have cultivated. There isn't that ongoing and personal awareness of God's voice. The one thing that God asks of His people is this: That we listen and obey His voice."[1]

This principle – of absolute obedience to God – has always applied to all who claim to follow the God of the Bible, both in the Old and New Testaments: "For I did not speak to your fathers or command them in the day that I brought them out of the land of Egypt, concerning burnt offerings and sacrifices. But this is what I commanded them, saying, 'Obey My voice and I will be your God and you shall be My people' " (Jeremiah 7:22-23). "The first thing He had in mind," said Derek Prince, "was not the keeping of the Law, or the offering of sacrifices, but listening to and obeying His voice."

This principle in the Old Testament is exactly the same in the New. "Jesus sums it up in one single verse," said Derek Prince. "In John 10:27, 'My sheep hear My voice and I know them and they follow Me.' The mark that we belong to Jesus is not that we follow a certain denominational pattern of life, or that we worship in a building, but that we hear His voice and hearing His voice, we follow Him in obedience."[2]

All of our religious rituals and attendance at Christian meetings count for little, if we are not hearing from God the Holy Spirit and obeying His voice! The Prophet Samuel asked, "Has the Lord as great delight in burnt offerings and sacrifices, as in obeying the voice of the Lord? Behold, to obey is better than sacrifice and to heed than the fat of rams" (1 Samuel 15:22). Therefore hearing God and obeying His voice is what counts to God. As Jesus said, "If you love Me, obey My commands" (John 14:15). Therefore, our obedience is the evidence that we love God. If there is no evidence in our lives of obedience, then there is no love for Him in us! Whatever He tells you to do, do it! Jesus said, "You are My friends, if you do whatever I command you" (John 15:14).

'The prime weakness of the Church today is its failure to honour the Holy Ghost,' wrote Michael Harper. 'How can we seek to know more of the truth and glory in our theology, when we do not honour the Spirit of Truth – sent by the Son to lead us into all truth?'[3]

Speaking of Jesus' teaching on the importance of the work of the Holy Spirit, Rees Howells explained that a revelation of faith from the Spirit of God can bring exactly the same blessing, as if Jesus' Himself had said it to us: "Faith inspired by the Holy Spirit will bring the same blessing as people received from being with the Lord Jesus." How is this possible? Because when the Holy Spirit speaks, the unity of the Trinity is expressed, as both the Father and the Son are speaking to us. "Whatever He hears He will speak," said Jesus, and "all things that the Father has are Mine, therefore He will take what is Mine and declare it to you" (John 16:13-15).

One lesson that Rees Howells' son, Samuel Rees Howells taught, is that there is a big difference between information and revelation. Today we have access to information and spiritual education, which is far beyond our level of obedience. We can speak convincingly on many spiritual subjects, based on what we have learnt from the revelations other people have received from the Holy Spirit. But head knowledge can lead to pride because 'knowledge puffs up' (1 Corinthians 8:1), and 'God resists the proud, but gives grace to the humble' (James 4:6). Meanwhile, direct revelation from God leads to humility, as we learn how little we really know! Let's be honest – we don't really know anything that we are not living! How many Christians know all there is to know about forgiveness, yet are still unforgiving? Meanwhile when the Holy Spirit teaches us, He tells us to live what we have learnt!

After Jesus' resurrection, He commissioned His followers to "make disciples of all nations" (Matthew 28:19). Then Jesus explained what a disciple is. According to Christ disciples are people who have been taught "to observe all things that I have commanded you" (Matthew 28:20). A disciple of Jesus Christ is not someone who believes in Him, but someone who obeys Him! How strange it must be for God to listen to our worship songs declaring how much we love Jesus, whilst we ignore much of what He has taught about how to live our lives (Matthew 16:24-26, Luke 14:26-35, Acts 11:26).

"I know what the plan of God for your life is," said one preacher.

"I'm not talking about the 'ministry' you have been called to. I'm talking about the plan God has for your life. God's plan for you is to get to know the Holy Spirit. God's plan is for you to know the Holy Spirit's voice and leading. God's plan is for you to draw near to God and allow the Holy Spirit to reveal Christ in you. God's plan is for you to love Him with all your heart, mind, will and strength. If you think God's ultimate purposes for your life concerns a title, ministry, or pulpit etc., then you have been gravely misled. You have been called to walk with the Lord by the Person of the Holy Spirit. Then out of that relationship, He may for a season lead you to 'a ministry,' but it is never the destination. The destination is to know Christ by the Spirit, whom He sent to reveal Christ in us – the hope of glory.

"But there are grave warnings from Church history, which we must heed. If we do not know the Holy Spirit, we will appoint ourselves to lives without God, and possibly even to a title, ministry or a pulpit! We may be called of God, but if we do not follow the Holy Spirit's leading we will supersede that call. We will appoint ourselves and we may not even know it! We will tell others we are following Christ, but in truth we are lost and outside of His will. If we do this, we will unknowingly reject the Spirit of God by our indifference, and Christ may reject us, as we have rejected Him. Remember it was Jesus Christ in heaven who warned Christians that names can be blotted out from the *Book of Life* and He can take away their lampstands, which means close their churches (Revelation 1:20, 2:5, 3:5). How many churches have closed today, because they have rejected the Spirit of God – the only Person who can reveal Christ in them?

"So what is our response today? Some people may hear what has been said and will make seeking an intimate relationship with the Holy Spirit a priority in their lives. But there are others who may say, 'That was a good message,' but will forget it and will not apply it. Then perhaps in ten or twenty years from now, after they have been round the same mountain in Egypt again and again, they will finally seek the Lord for the breakthrough they need; and what will the Lord say to them? The Lord will repeat to them what you are hearing today. 'Get to know the Holy Spirit. He is the One I sent to be your Teacher and Guide.' So why waste ten or twenty years of your life? Why seek a title, ministry or pulpit, when you've been called to get to know Jesus Christ, by the only Person who knows Jesus Christ in all His fullness?"

In our Christian lives we can walk in the Spirit or in the flesh (Galatians 5:16). Jesus warned, "That which is born of the flesh is flesh and that which is born of the Spirit is spirit" (John 3:6). This means we can be in the flesh or in the Spirit in every area of our lives! This includes all counterfeit conversions in churches and all the 'good works' which were birthed by the power of the flesh, without the leading of the Spirit. It also includes ministries founded by God, which have gone astray from the Holy Spirit, as they begin to rely on human abilities. We have made many nominal Christians and tainted ministries by the hand of the flesh, now it is time to make disciples of Jesus Christ by the leading of the Holy Spirit!

Rees Howells used to say, "There is only One Person alive on earth today, who is a witness to the resurrection of Christ and that Person is the Holy Ghost." Why then are we seeking everything else, other than a close and intimate relationship with the Holy Spirit? He will make us live like Christ, because He was a witness to Christ's life on earth, and it was He who filled and anointed Christ for His ministry. If you want Christ – receive the Person of the Holy Spirit. If you want the Father and the Son – receive the Holy Spirit!

Scholars tell us that if one phrase is repeated three times in the Bible, it is because God wants to place special emphasis on the message. Therefore imagine the importance of a six-fold witness! In the book of Revelation, we have a six-fold witness and warning from the mouth of Jesus Christ, for the Church to listen to what the Holy Spirit says: "Whoever has ears, let them hear what the Spirit says to the churches" (Revelation 2:7). The exact same phrase is then repeated another five times! (Revelation 2:17, 2:29, 3:6, 3:13, 3:22). This six-fold witness represents one of the last direct messages Christ gave to His Church in the Bible – "Hear what the Spirit says!" Then, in preparation for the end times, it is the Spirit and the Church who speak as one, to expect and welcome Christ's return to earth. 'The Spirit and the bride say, "Come!" ' (Revelation 22:17).

For generations churches have been making 'good Christians.' We urge people to confess a vague faith in Christ, join a church and sit in the pew. How many times have we heard this: "If you want to become a Christian tonight, all you have to do is pray this quick and simple prayer?" Then when people hesitate, the preacher states, "Don't worry, it's just a quick prayer, repeat these words after me." The confession of the prayer may be biblically accurate, but does becoming a disciple of Jesus Christ – turning from darkness to light, to become a new creation, really involve repeating a few phrases, without understanding them, or showing any sign of conviction of sin, purging repentance and red-hot faith? We need the Spirit of God and the Holy Spirit needs vessels fit for His purposes. Will you become one?

*Questions to consider:* Have you acknowledged your need? Have you asked the Holy Spirit to make Jesus Christ your Lord?

*Actions:* Confess your need and ask God to make you His vessel.

# Chapter Forty-Six

## Resisting the Holy Spirit

- 'But, as he who was born according to the flesh then persecuted him who was born according to the Spirit, even so it is now' (Galatians 4:29).
- Peter said, "Ananias, why has Satan filled your heart to lie to the Holy Spirit and keep back part of the price of the land for yourself?" (Acts 5:3).
- Stephen said, "You stiff-necked and uncircumcised in heart and ears! You always resist the Holy Spirit; as your fathers did, so do you" (Acts 7:51).
- 'When Simon saw that through the laying on of the apostles' hands the Holy Spirit was given, he offered them money, saying, "Give me this power also, that anyone on whom I lay hands may receive the Holy Spirit." But Peter said to him, "Your money perish with you, because you thought that the gift of God could be purchased with money! You have neither part nor portion in this matter, for your heart is not right in the sight of God. Repent therefore of this your wickedness, and pray God if perhaps the thought of your heart may be forgiven you. For I see that you are poisoned by bitterness and bound by iniquity" ' (Acts 8:18-23).
- 'Elymas the sorcerer withstood them, seeking to turn the proconsul away from the faith. Then Saul, who also is called Paul, filled with the Holy Spirit, looked intently at him and said, "O full of all deceit and all fraud, you son of the devil, you enemy of all righteousness, will you not cease perverting the straight ways of the Lord? And now, indeed, the hand of the Lord is upon you, and you shall be blind, not seeing the sun for a time." And immediately a dark mist fell on him, and he went around seeking someone to lead him by the hand' (Acts 13:8-11).
- 'As the Holy Spirit says, "Today, if you will hear His voice, do not harden your hearts as in the rebellion, in the day of trial in the wilderness, where your fathers tested Me" ' (Hebrews 3:7-9).
- 'For it is impossible for those who were once enlightened, and have tasted the heavenly gift, and have become partakers of the Holy Spirit, and have tasted the good Word of God and the powers of the age to come, if they fall away, to renew them again to repentance, since they crucify again for themselves the Son of God, and put Him to an open shame' (Hebrews 6:4-6).

## Chapter Forty-Seven

## Let the Spirit Possess You

"Many people have put their faith in Jesus Christ and received the baptism of the Holy Spirit, but have never progressed from there," said a disciple of the Lord. "They claim to know God, but in truth they have only had their first introduction to Him and He continues to be almost a complete stranger to them. To overcome this problem they must resolve to get to know the Person of the Holy Spirit. Jesus came to baptise us with the Holy Spirit and fire (Luke 3:16); why then have many never experienced the fire? The reason is because the baptism of the Holy Spirit is refreshing and empowering, but to walk in the greater works of Jesus (John 14:12), we must go through the fire and allow Him to burn up our sinful works and flesh lives. Many will run here and there thinking they can catch an anointing, like a butterfly caught in a net, but this is like chasing after the wind. You cannot catch an anointing on the cheap, you have to pay the full price to walk in God's power, just like Elisha paid the full price to walk in Elijah's anointing (1 Kings 19:19-21).

"Some believe this special anointing and intimate relationship with the Holy Spirit that D.L. Moody, Rees Howells, Evan Roberts, Duncan Campbell, Samuel Rees Howells and many other servants of the Lord had were unique, and are impossible for us to have. But this is not true. All our callings are different, but we can all be as close to the Holy Spirit as we choose to be. We can know the Holy Spirit possessing us, in a similar way as Rees Howells etc., when we too are prepared to pay the same price they paid to draw aside and be crucified with Christ. We don't need any more wishbone – 'I wish I had a relationship with God like them,' we need backbone – 'I will seek and obey God like they did.' What about you?"

"I can't stress this point enough," said a disciple of the Lord. "Jesus Christ is in heaven and the Holy Spirit is the One who continues God's work on earth. Luke wrote of Jesus: 'Whom heaven must receive until the times of restoration of all things' (Acts 3:21), and Paul wrote we must 'wait for His Son from heaven' (1 Thessalonians 1:10). We love Jesus and we serve Jesus, but it is His Spirit, the Spirit of Christ (Philippians 1:19), who must live in us, to lead us into God's will. Jesus Christ is in heaven and He can only be present in a church meeting in the Person of the Spirit of Christ (Matthew 18:20). If the Spirit of Christ is not there, God is not there. Remember, we are being 'built together for a dwelling place of God in the Spirit' (Ephesians 2:22).

"We must all welcome the Spirit of Christ into our lives and in our churches. If He is not living and working through us, we are not the Church. Two thousand years ago, Jesus told His Church He was going away to heaven saying, 'It is to your advantage that I go away, for if I do not go away, the Helper will not come to you; but if I depart, I will send Him to you' (John 16:7). Jesus Christ could only be in one place on earth, but the Holy Spirit can be everywhere and in every believer who welcomes Him.

"For two thousand years Jesus Christ has been interceding in heaven (Romans 8:34, Hebrews 7:25), meanwhile the Holy Spirit has been and is on earth, seeking to indwell believers to glorify Jesus. The Lord gave us a very detailed description of the work of the Holy Spirit recorded in John chapters 14-17, and Paul wrote a whole chapter on the ministry of the Holy Spirit in Romans 8. Why then do we hear little about the Spirit in many churches? We know more about Jesus, who left earth two millennia ago, than the Spirit who has been living and working in the Church for the same period!

"What will the Spirit show us? He will show us how divided our hearts have been and how unfaithful we have been to Jesus Christ. When the Holy Spirit came into my life in a powerful way, He showed me an image of my heart, divided into various sections (Jeremiah 17:9-10, Revelation 2:23). As I considered this image of my divided heart, with all the various sections loyal to the various desires of the world, the flesh and the devil, and with a little segment loyal to God, He revealed my true self (Romans 7:18). He proved that Jesus Christ was Lord of only a very small section of my deeply divided heart, and it was His will to breakdown every division in my heart and fill it with Himself.

"After moving in the gifts of the Spirit I had told people I was filled with the Spirit, but He taught me that most of my heart was still filled with self, ambition, greed and other sins. He came to me as God and told me He wanted every area of my heart, and it was His will to take full possession of every area of me – my heart, soul, spirit and body. My life had to go and His life had to enter into my vessel.

"Let me stress this point: Imagine a picture of a heart, divided into numerous sections, with various 'lords' of each segment. This is what the Lord showed me from Paul's letter to the Galatians. 'Now the works of the flesh are evident, which are: adultery, fornication, uncleanness, lewdness, idolatry, sorcery, hatred, contentions, jealousies, outbursts of wrath, selfish ambitions, dissensions, heresies, envy, murders, drunkenness, revelries, and the like...' (Galatians 5:19-21). He showed me my heart was like this list above and the Holy Spirit would not come in and fill those areas, unless I repented. I had to empty them before He could enter in all His fullness. He told me He wanted to replace those sections of my heart named with all those sins, with the fruit of the Holy Spirit:

'Love, joy, peace, longsuffering, kindness, goodness, faithfulness, gentleness and self-control' (Galatians 5:22-23).

"He is the Spirit of Holiness and He showed me that He wants me to reflect the holiness of my Lord. As the Bible states: 'Therefore, having these promises, beloved, let us cleanse ourselves from all filthiness of the flesh and spirit, perfecting holiness in the fear of God' (2 Corinthians 7:1), and, 'Pursue peace with all people, and holiness, without which no one will see the Lord' (Hebrews 12:14).

"As I began to surrender further areas of my heart to the Lord Jesus and allow the Holy Spirit to purge me of worldliness, self and sin, my new Holy Spirit life was a challenge to many 'nice,' but indifferent Christians. Some of them rebutted me and said, 'Be careful you don't become so holy, that you are of no earthly good.' As I reflected upon this, I realised this kind of advice is nothing more than the infiltration of Satan in the minds of Christians. Did Jesus ever say in the gospels, "Now, be careful that you don't become too holy?" No! Jesus was filled with the Spirit, and so were His disciples and people flocked to hear because God was working in them.

"When Christians warn other believers about becoming too holy, this is an excuse to remain in sin and stay worldly, but John told us: 'Do not love the world or the things in the world. If anyone loves the world, the love of the Father is not in him. For all that is in the world – the lust of the flesh, the lust of the eyes, and the pride of life – is not of the Father but is of the world' (1 John 2:15-17).

"Too many Christians have become addicted to empty tradition, to ceremony and have become religious. Your relationship should be with Jesus, by His Spirit, not with a religion, church or denomination. We don't need to meet the world on its compromised ground, we need to meet God, and as Christ is lifted up in our lives, He will draw all men to Himself. But first you need to meet the Holy Spirit as a Person, by climbing up your own Mount Moriah to offer the full sacrifice of your life. If you are prepared to pay the full price, the fire will fall, and the Person will descend upon you and live in you. 'But the cost is too great,' you may think. Yet, Jim Elliot (1927-1956), the martyred missionary to Ecuador said, 'He is no fool who gives what he cannot keep, to gain that which he cannot lose.' How will you respond to Christ's eternal call? Will you be a vessel of the Spirit?"

In his final conversation with Samuel Rees Howells, a staff member asked, "What do you think is the most important thing in our walk with God?" Samuel Rees Howells quietly and reverently replied, "Obedience to the Holy Spirit."

This book is also available as an ebook.

# Sources and Notes

Chapter 3
1. *Revival Fires and Awakenings* by Mathew Backholer, ByFaith Media, 2012, p.159.
2. *Real Religion – Revival Sermons Delivered During His Twentieth Visit to America* by Gipsy Smith, Hodder and Stoughton, 1922, p.132.
3. *Revival Sermons in Outline* edited by Perren, Revell, 1894, pp.73-74.

Chapter 5
1. *The Great Dynamic* by Gideon L. Powell, The Christian Witness Company, 1923, pp. 87-88.
2. *Mighty Moments* by Lionel B. Fletcher, Religious Tract Society, 1931, pp.15-16.
3. *The Enduement of Power* by Oswald J. Smith, Marshall, Morgan & Scott, 1933, 1937, p.81.

Chapter 7
1. *Ye Shall Receive Power From on High – A Bible Study on the Baptism in the Holy Spirit* by Gwen Shaw, Engeltal Press, 1987, p.1.
2. *Mighty Moments* by Lionel B. Fletcher, Religious Tract Society, 1931, pp.15-16.
3. The Fullness of the Spirit by Rev. Evan Hopkins, Llandrindod Convention, Wales, UK, 1906.

Chapter 9
1. *Revival Fires and Awakenings* by Mathew Backholer, ByFaith Media, 2012, p.75.
2. *Always Abounding, An Intimate Sketch of Oswald J. Smith of Toronto* by J. Edwin Orr, Marshall, Morgan & Scott, 1948, pp.12, 30.
3. *God's Hell and Other Addresses* by William P. Nicholson, Marshall, Morgan & Scott, c.1930, p.142.
4. *The Evangelist – His Ministry and Message* by W.P. Nicholson, Marshal Morgan & Scott, c.1940, p.86.

Chapter 11
1. *Real Religion – Revival Sermons Delivered During His Twentieth Visit to America* by Gipsy Smith, Hodder and Stoughton, 1922, p.122.
2. *The Great Dynamic* by Gideon L. Powell, The Christian Witness Company, 1923, pp.58-59.

Chapter 13
1. *Life in the Spirit* by John White, London Epworth Press, 1976, p.45.

Chapter 15
1. God Challenges Job part 4 by Derek Prince, Legacy Radio, 14 September 2012.
2. *Samuel Rees Howells: A Life of Intercession* by Richard Maton, ByFaith Media, 2012, p.132.
3. The Fullness of the Spirit by Rev. Evan Hopkins, Llandrindod Convention, UK, 1906.

Chapter 17
1. *Occult Bondage and Deliverance by* Dr. Kurt Koch, Kregel Publications, 1972.
2. *Full Salvation* by J.A. Broadbelt, Marshall, Morgan & Scott, 1936, p.67.

Chapter 19
1. The Power of the Spirit by Derek Prince, Legacy Radio, 16 August 2012.

Chapter 21
1. The Fullness of the Spirit by Rev. Evan Hopkins, Llandrindod Convention, Wales, UK, 1906.
2. *God's Answers, Revival Sermons* by Duncan Campbell, the Faith Mission, 1960, p.14.
3. *The Great Dynamic* by Gideon L. Powell, The Christian Witness Company, 1923, pp.7, 16-18.

Chapter 23
1. *The Enduement of Power* by Oswald J. Smith, Marshall, Morgan & Scott, 1933, p.40.
2. *The Revival We Need* by Oswald J. Smith, Marshall, Morgan & Scott, 1940, p.86.
3. *Spirit of Revival* by I.R. Govan, the Faith Mission, 1938, 1978, p.177.

Chapter 25
1. *Annals of The Early Friends* by Frances Anne Budge, Henry Longstreth, Philadelphia, 1900, p.134.
2. *The Focused Life* by E.C.W. Boulton, Elim Publishing Company, 1932, p.2.
3. *The Focused Life* by E.C.W. Boulton, Elim Publishing Company, 1932, p.48.
4. *Christ the Healer* by F.F. Bosworth, Chosen, 1924, 2008, p.163.
5. *Can God – 10,000 Miles of Miracle in Britain* by J. Edwin Orr, Marshall, Morgan & Scott, 1934, p.113.

Chapter 27
1. *I Believe in the Holy Ghost* by Maynard James, Bettany Fellowship, 1965, p.66.
2. *The Scarlet Sin and Other Revival Sermons* by John R. Rice, Sword Of The Lord Publishers, 1946, pp.234-235.
3. *When Iron Gates Yield* by Geoffrey T. Bull, Hodder and Stoughton, 1955, 1965, pp.98-99.
4. The Fullness of the Spirit by Rev. Evan Hopkins, Llandrindod Convention, Wales, UK, 1906.
5. *Revival in Our Time* edited by F.A. Tatford, The Paternoster Press, 1947, p.47.
6. *The Price and Power of Revival* by Duncan Campbell, Faith Mission, 1962, p.53.

Chapter 29
1. *Mere Christianity* by C.S. Lewis, Christian Behaviour, Geoffrey Bles, 1952, p.37.
2. *Mere Christianity* by C.S. Lewis, Faith, Geoffrey Bles, 1952, p.68.
3. *I Believe in the Holy Ghost* by Maynard James, Bettany Fellowship, 1965, p.146.
4. The Fullness of the Spirit by Rev. Evan Hopkins, Llandrindod Convention, Wales, UK, 1906.
5. *Revival in Our Time* edited by F.A. Tatford, The Paternoster Press, 1947, pp.28, 30-32.
6. *The Great Dynamic* by Gideon L. Powell, The Christian Witness Company, 1923, pp.89-90.

Chapter 31
1. *Mere Christianity* by C.S. Lewis, Geoffrey Bles, 1952, pp.95-96.
2. *The Price of Revival* by John D. Drysdale, C. Tinling & Co, 1946, p.183.
3. The Fullness of the Spirit by Rev. Evan Hopkins, Llandrindod, Wales, UK, 1906.
4. *As At The Beginning, The Twentieth Century Pentecostal Revival* by Michael Harper, Hodder and Stoughton, 1965, p.24.

Chapter 33
1. *Samuel Rees Howells: A Life of Intercession* by Richard Maton, ByFaith Media, 2012, p.225.

Chapter 35
1. *The Dynamic of Service* by A. Paget Wilkes, Japan Evangelistic Band, 1925, p.307.
2. *Revival an Enquiry* by Max Warren, SCM Press, 1954, p.14.

Chapter 37
1. The Fullness of the Spirit by Rev. Evan Hopkins, Llandrindod, Wales, UK, 1906.

Chapter 41
*The Person and Work of the Holy Spirit* by R.A. Torrey, Fleming H. Revel Company, 1910, p.129.

Chapter 43
1. *Sermons of Thomas Arnold*, Part 1, B. Fellows, 1845, p.339.

Chapter 45
1. Spiritual Benefits of Redemption by Derek Prince, Legacy Radio, 19 June 2012.
2. Spiritual Benefits of Redemption by Derek Prince, Legacy Radio, 19 June 2012.
3. *As At The Beginning, The Twentieth Century Pentecostal Revival* by Michael Harper, Hodder and Stoughton, 1965, p.96.

# ByFaith Media Books

***Revival Fires and Awakenings – Thirty-Six Visitations of the Holy Spirit*** by Mathew Backholer.

***Reformation to Revival, 500 Years of God's Glory: Sixty Revivals, Awakenings and Heaven-Sent Visitations of the Holy Spirit*** by Mathew Backholer

***How to Plan, Prepare and Successfully Complete Your Short-Term Mission*** by Mathew Backholer.

***Revival Fire – 150 Years of Revivals*** by Mathew Backholer documents twelve revivals from ten countries.

***Discipleship for Everyday Living*** by Mathew Backholer. A dynamic biblical book for Christian growth.

***Global Revival, Worldwide Outpourings, Forty-Three Visitations of the Holy Spirit*** by Mathew Backholer.

***Understanding Revival and Addressing the Issues it Provokes*** by Mathew Backholer.

***Extreme Faith – On Fire Christianity*** by Mathew Backholer. Powerful foundations for faith in Christ!

***Revival Answers: True and False Revivals*** by Mathew Backholer. What is genuine and false revival?

***Short-Term Missions, A Christian Guide to STMs***, *For Leaders, Pastors, Students…*by Mathew Backholer.

***Budget Travel, A Guide to Travelling on a Shoestring Explore the World, A Discount Overseas Adventure Trip: Gap Year, Backpacking*** by Mathew Backholer

***Prophecy Now, Prophetic Words and Divine Revelations, For You, the Church and the Nations*** by Michael Backholer.

***Samuel Rees Howells: A Life of Intercession*** by Richard Maton. Learn how intercession and prayer changed history.

*Samuel, Son and Successor of Rees Howells* by Richard Maton. Discover the full biography of Samuel Rees Howells.

*The Holy Spirit in a Man* by R.B. Watchman. An autobiography.

*Tares and Weeds in your Church: Trouble & Deception in God's House* by R.B. Watchman.

*How Christianity Made the Modern World* by Paul Backholer.

*Holy Spirit Power: Knowing the Voice, Guidance and Person of the Holy Spirit* by Paul Backholer.

*Heaven: A Journey to Paradise and the Heavenly City* by Paul Backholer.

*The Exodus Evidence In Pictures – The Bible's Exodus* by Paul Backholer. 100+ colour photos.

*The Ark of the Covenant – Investigating the Ten Leading Claims* by Paul Backholer. 80+ colour photos.

*Jesus Today, Daily Devotional: 100 Days with Jesus Christ* by Paul Backholer.

*Britain, A Christian Country* by Paul Backholer.

*Celtic Christianity and the First Christian Kings in Britain* by Paul Backholer.

*The Baptism of Fire, Personal Revival and the Anointing for Supernatural Living* by Paul Backholer.

*Glimpses of Glory, Revelations in the Realms of God* by Paul Backholer

*Lost Treasures of the Bible* by Paul Backholer.

*The End Times: A Journey Through the Last Days. The Book of Revelation*…by Paul Backholer.

*Debt Time Bomb! Debt Mountains: The Financial Crisis and its Toxic Legacy* by Paul Backholer. Ebook.

**www.ByFaithBooks.co.uk**

# ByFaith Media DVDs

*Great Christian Revivals* on 1 DVD is an uplifting account of some of the greatest revivals in Church history. Filmed on location across Britain and drawing upon archive information, the stories of the Welsh Revival (1904-1905), the Hebridean Revival (1949-1952) and the Evangelical Revival (1739-1791), are told in this 72 minute documentary.

*ByFaith – Quest for the Ark of the Covenant* on 1 DVD. Experience an adventure and investigate the mystery of the lost Ark of the Covenant! Explore Ethiopia's rock churches; find the Egyptian Pharaoh who entered Solomon's Temple and search for the Queen of Sheba's Palace. Four episodes. 100+ minutes.

*ByFaith – World Mission* on 1 DVD. Pack your backpack and join two adventurers as they travel through 14 nations on their global short-term mission (STM). Get inspired for your STM, as you watch this 85 minute adventure; filmed over three years.

*Israel in Egypt – The Exodus Mystery* on 1 DVD. A four year quest searching for the evidence for Joseph, Moses and the Hebrew Slaves in Egypt. Explore the Exodus route, hunt for the Red Sea and climb Mount Sinai. This is the best of the eight episode TV series *ByFaith – In Search of the Exodus.* 110+ minutes.

*ByFaith – In Search of the Exodus* on 2 DVDs. The quest to find the evidence for ancient Israel in Egypt, the Red Sea and Mount Sinai, in eight TV episodes. 200+ minutes.

Visit **www.ByFaith.org** to watch the trailers for
these DVDs and for more information.

**www.ByFaithDVDs.co.uk**

# Notes

CPSIA information can be obtained
at www.ICGtesting.com
Printed in the USA
LVHW081627080821
694842LV00014B/631

9 781907 066566